100 Ideas for Secondary Teachers:

Supporting EAL Learners

Other titles in the 100 Ideas for Secondary Teachers series:

100 Ideas for Secondary Teachers:

Supporting EAL Learners

Catharine Driver and Chris Pim

BLOOMSBURY EDUCATION

LONDON   OXFORD   NEW YORK   NEW DELHI   SYDNEY

BLOOMSBURY EDUCATION
Bloomsbury Publishing Plc
50 Bedford Square, London, WC1B 3DP, UK
29 Earlsfort Terrace, Dublin 2, Ireland

BLOOMSBURY, BLOOMSBURY EDUCATION and
the Diana logo are trademarks of Bloomsbury Publishing Plc

First published in Great Britain, 2018 by Bloomsbury Education

A catalogue record for this book is available from the British Library

ISBN: PB: 978-1-4729-5411-4; ePub: 978-1-4729-5413-8;
ePDF: 978-1-4729-5412-1

2 4 6 8 10 9 7 5 3 1

Typeset by Newgen KnowledgeWorks Pvt. Ltd., Chennai, India
Printed and bound by CPI Group (UK) Ltd., Croydon, CR0 4YY

To find out more about our authors and books visit
www.bloomsbury.com and sign up for our newsletters.

Contents

Introduction

By the time most EAL learners arrive in secondary school, their subject knowledge and literacy are already in place and these concepts transfer into English well once prior knowledge is activated. This is especially true for learners who have age-appropriate literacy in their first language. Teachers and other adults working with EAL learners need to draw on a student's L1 skills to support learning right across the curriculum. Students arriving mid-phase and late into KS4 can present particular challenges. Schools will need to be flexible in their approach to ensure that practice and provision are in the best interests of the young person. While acquisition of English for academic purposes is an important element, schools must also take account of the wider aspects of a young person's development and their longer-term aspirations for the future.

In the United Kingdom, the accepted position regarding EAL teaching and learning is that students best acquire English within the context of the curriculum and in the mainstream classroom. It's generally true that what is good practice for EAL learners will be good practice for all.

To communicate well with all staff, it's helpful to use a set of well-established terms to talk about where students are in their acquisition of English. These terms are not linked to formal assessment. They relate to how long a student has been learning English, their competence across the four skills of reading, writing, speaking and listening and what research and experience tells us about how long it might take to acquire English for a range of purposes across the curriculum. Therefore, in our description of how the 100 ideas in this book relate to students at different stages in their acquisition of English, we make specific reference to:

- **Beginner EAL learners** – young people who are new to English and also those who have acquired some English, either in their country of origin or as a result of studying for up to two years in the United Kingdom. Towards the end of a two-year period, they are likely to exhibit reasonable oral skills and may be reading quite well but still need a lot of support for writing.
- **Developing EAL learners** – young people who have been in the UK education system for two to four years and have established competence in oral language. They operate confidently in most classroom situations, but may struggle with extended reading

and writing because they lack the wide vocabulary and advanced grammatical structures required for high attainment across the curriculum.

- **Advanced EAL learners** – those who either have had extensive English teaching abroad, perhaps in English-medium schools, or have been studying English for several years in the United Kingdom. These learners will generally have well-developed oral skills, can read and write competently and will eventually reach, or in many cases exceed, the attainment level of their monolingual peers across the curriculum.

Both developing and advanced learners tend to plateau at transition points in their education (e.g. Years 7 and Years 9/10) and often require specific teaching strategies and support to move them on in their learning.

About this book

This book will be essential reading for trainees on initial teacher training programmes as well as for more experienced staff working as teachers, teaching assistants or in other support roles in the school.

This new edition has been written specifically for a secondary phase audience. The 100 ideas contained within these pages aim to be both practical and simple to implement. At the same time, each idea represents a challenge to the reader. It may reinforce already-held beliefs, giving confidence in the support you already offer to EAL learners, and encourage you to take provision to the next stage. It may, however, require an adjustment in your thinking, resulting in alternative approaches around school and in the classroom. Finally, we hope that each idea has been articulated so succinctly that it will be obvious to you what further action needs to be taken in your own school context to bring the idea to fruition.

As you will see, the book has been organised into different sections. The earlier sections deal with the challenge of how to settle, assess and make provision for new EAL students, especially those newly arrived from abroad. The middle sections focus on effective teaching and learning and will be relevant to all subject teachers. The sections towards the end of the book illustrate how important it is to take a holistic view in meeting the needs of EAL learners. Effective whole-school provision involves all staff, whatever their role in the school. These sections will be particularly relevant for EAL coordinators and other senior managers in the school.

Catharine Driver and Chris Pim

Acronyms

AfL	Assessment for Learning
BICS	Basic Interpersonal Communication Skill
BAME	Black, Asian and Minority Ethnic (also known as BME)
CALP	Cognitive Academic Language Proficiency
CPD	Continuing Professional Development
DARTs	Directed Activities Related to Texts
EAL	English as an Additional Language
EMA	Ethnic Minority Achievement
ESL	English as a Second Language
ESOL	English for Speakers of Other Languages (post-16 in UK)
ILP	Individual Language Plan
IELTS	International English Language Test System
IWB	Interactive Whiteboard
KS3	Key Stage 3 (ages 11–14)
KS4	Key Stage 4 (ages 14–16)
KWL	What I Know, What I Want to Know, What I Have Learned
LSA	Learning Support Assistant
L1	First Language
L2	Second Language
SEND	Special Educational Needs and Disability
SLT	Senior Leadership Team
TA	Teaching Assistant
VC	Videoconference
WBRI	White British

How to use this book

This book includes quick, easy and practical ideas for you to dip in and out of, to help you provide the best support possible to EAL learners in the secondary classroom.

Each idea includes:

- a catchy title, easy to refer to and share with your colleagues
- an interesting quote linked to the idea
- a summary of the idea in bold, making it easy to flick through the book and identify an idea you want to use at a glance
- a step-by-step guide to implementing an idea.

Each idea also includes one or more of the following:

Teaching tip

Practical tips and advice for how and how not to run the activity or put the idea into practice.

Taking it further

Ideas and advice for how to extend the idea or develop it further.

Bonus idea ★

There are 59 bonus ideas in this book that are extra exciting, extra original and extra interesting.

Share how you use these ideas and find out what other practitioners have done using **#100ideas**.

Online resources also accompany this book. When online resources are referenced in the book, follow the link, www.bloomsbury.com/100-ideas-secondary-eal, to find extra resources.

Induction and transition

Part 1

School information and induction materials

'Experience tells me that newly-arrived families from black and minority ethnic backgrounds often face linguistic and cultural barriers that can inhibit full access to school-based information.'

The additional cost of customising websites and induction booklets for speakers and readers of other languages will be well worth it. Parents will value accessible school information whatever their country of origin.

Many schools produce a prospectus and induction materials for new students and their families. If this information is already available at your school, adapt these materials further to reflect the major ethnic and linguistic groups within the local community and to help cater for the needs of families that have recently arrived from abroad.

Where possible, translate the essential elements of the information available, although this may only be possible for the larger minority groups within the school. Bear in mind that some parents or carers may not be fully literate in their first language and so will not be able to access written translations. You could release school information through bilingual podcasts and videos hosted on the school's website.

Families who are new to the United Kingdom may be unfamiliar with school processes in this country, and while we should be cautious about generalising, it can be useful to clearly state the school's position on various matters.

It is helpful to communicate the following information:

- Explain that all learners must study the full National Curriculum as well as stating the school's position on typically occurring issues such as religious education and worship and sex and relationships education.
- Offer clear guidance on homework for each year group (since some families expect more than the recommended amount).
- Identify the best and worst times to go on holiday or take extended family visits to the home country.
- Help parents to have appropriate and equitable career aspirations for all their children.
- Extend a clear invitation for families to be fully involved in all aspects of school life (in some countries it is not traditional to have significant school contact).
- Provide clear explanations of what it means to have special educational needs and disabilities (SEND), as some parents or carers find this 'diagnosis' hard to accept for their child.
- Explain the importance of accurately recording their child's ethnicity and spoken language on the admissions form.

Taking it further

It might be a good idea to release school information through bilingual podcasts and videos hosted on the school's website.

Conduct an in-depth admissions interview

'Many parents find entering a secondary school intimidating and this can be especially true for those who are new to the country and where they are not fully proficient in English.'

The initial meeting with a family can make all the difference to how a student settles into a new school and it is vital that schools think about how to ensure a positive first experience and facilitate a strong relationship in the longer term.

Plan in advance who will conduct admissions interviews with the parents or carers of a newly arrived EAL learner and how best to obtain important background information.

Here are some tips to help you to prepare for an admissions interview:

- Invite all parents/carers and the learner to the meeting several days in advance; ask if they will need an interpreter.
- Invitation letters should be followed up with phone calls using the student's L1 where possible.
- When an interpreter is necessary, arrange for one to be present during the meeting.
- Brief interpreters before the meeting, and provide them with copies of paperwork such as school admission forms and questionnaires in advance.
- Allow additional time for filling in the application and consent forms before the interview.
- Be flexible about interview timing, as both parents may be working. Some families will have childcare requirements, as they may not have typical family support networks.
- Note that in some Muslim families, a male adult may need to accompany the mother or female carer.

During the meeting:

- Be aware that greeting customs can vary across cultures, and some adults may choose not to shake hands upon first meeting.
- Seating should be arranged informally.
- When an interpreter is involved, always direct questions to the family members, maintain eye contact and gesture liberally to reinforce meaning.
- Work through a set of prepared questions, and make notes as the meeting progresses; it can help to explain that the information will be confidential to the school, except where there is a required child-protection disclosure.
- Ensure there is ample opportunity for the parents or carers to ask any immediate questions about the school.

Bonus idea ★

At the end of the meeting, establish a date with parents or carers to provide feedback as to how their child has settled in at the school and review progress again ideally with an interpreter.

Gathering information and assessing prior learning

'EAL learners are not a homogenous group; the only factor that unites them is that English is not their first language. Therefore, making general assumptions about them should be avoided.'

To inform practice and provision for each learner, schools need to collect as much information as possible at the point of entry. Parents/carers and children are an integral part of this process.

As previously mentioned, it is important to gather background information about newly arrived learners as soon as possible after they start school. Try to capture details about previous schooling, e.g. what subjects have or have not been studied. Science subjects may not have been taught in less developed countries. Find out about proficiency in L1 and pertinent medical, social and cultural issues. Other useful evidence includes end-of-year reports and samples of work from the country of origin.

It is not appropriate to run a battery of tests with a new EAL learner. A short oral assessment of English and basic maths should be sufficient at first and this should take place *before* the admission day so that teachers have time to allocate groups and print a timetable. Continue to make observations and talk to the student in class while they are settling in, and after a week or two you can carry out some more formal testing. Reading tests are not recommended unless they are specifically designed for non-native speakers. Vocabulary size tests are better.

You will be able to obtain much of the required information at an in-depth admissions interview (Idea 2) with parents or carers.

Bonus idea ★

Some schools use an online background information collation tool to support this process. There is a handy online background collation tool at http://newarrivals.segfl.org.uk. Such a tool presents a series of typical questions through an online form, supported through L1 audio files. While responses are mainly made through tick boxes, and writing is kept to a minimum, it is recommended that a TA/LSA facilitates the use of the tool. Once complete, the system produces a written report in English that can be printed or saved and incorporated into a wider early profile.

Survival language

'Being able to use a few words and phrases in a new language can give new students some confidence, particularly with communicating basic needs.'

Survival language may be taught in the first few days of entry to a new school, but not at the expense of subject teaching. It can be learned naturally through student interaction and visual clues.

Build up a range of 'survival language' materials to support learners who are new to English. This will help them settle more easily and will enhance their interaction with adults and peers. Survival language introduces learners to essential vocabulary and simple phrases, e.g. greetings, numbers and classroom instructions such as 'write', 'read' or 'answer the question'. Common questions or phrases are also useful, e.g. 'I don't understand' and 'Where is the library?'

Survival language is best supported with images to help convey meaning. Vocabulary fans, booklets and wall displays are all good vehicles for packaging survival language for EAL learners. Learners who are literate in L1 will benefit from having dual-language versions, so they can transfer knowledge between languages. These learners should also be encouraged to keep a record of new language as it is encountered.

Remember, survival language does not need to be specifically taught, especially if it takes time out of the curriculum. It is intended to support learners both in and out of the classroom during their first few weeks at a new school and can be introduced in a couple of induction lessons when students arrive. Older learners will appreciate materials that are relatively sophisticated and supported by imagery with a more adult feel.

Teaching tip

Class and subject teachers should also prepare their class for a new EAL student by learning a few words in their language, and gathering useful resources, such as glossaries and dual-language dictionaries (Idea 26).

Bonus idea

Download some survival language booklets (with translations) to give to students, e.g. https://sites.google.com/a/edubuzz.org/english-as-an-additional-language/resources-in-polish.

Conduct a school language survey

'My teacher spoke to me in Turkish today. It really helped me feel welcome in class and I understood what the topic was about really easily.'

Conducting an audit of language use among the whole school community is a useful first step in terms of preparing for new arrivals.

Taking it further

Use resources from the Multilingual Manchester website to help you with the whole-school survey. See http://mlm. humanities.manchester. ac.uk/ for more details.

Use resources from the Multilingualism in Europe (LUCIDE) project for ideas for teacher training about multilingualism: www.urbanlanguages. eu/images/stories/ docs/toolkits/toolkit- plurilingual.pdf.

Over 16% of students (as of 2017) in English state-funded secondary schools are speakers of another language at home or in the community. Finding out about the languages used within the school community really helps schools develop the most effective provision for EAL learners and their families. This is important for EAL learners who were born in the United Kingdom as well as for new arrivals. Do you know all the languages spoken in your school? Is your school management information system (MIS) up to date with the full range of languages used by learners and their families?

Learning about other languages can help teachers capitalise on the linguistic knowledge and skills of their learners for embedding intercultural work within the curriculum, e.g. using words with similar roots (*condensation, condensación, kondensacja*) to learn vocabulary, as well as learning numerical methods from around the world.

Here are some points to help you conduct a whole-school language survey and record the results.

- Collaborate with the modern languages department, who may already conduct a language awareness survey at the start of each year. The European Day of Languages is celebrated on 26 September, and could be used to give the survey a whole-school focus.

- Include *all* staff in the survey. You may well find hidden talents!
- New-arrival EAL learners and their families will feel welcome if they see that the school has taken their language and cultural background into consideration. You will be able to create a list of students whose families need interpreters at parents' events.
- Finding out about the features of specific languages helps with initial assessments (Idea 10). Features to consider include the written script, writing directionality, punctuation, word order and numeric symbols, among others.
- Many learners will continue to learn their L1 at home or at community language schools and may well be able to take public examinations in the subject (Idea 86).

Bonus idea ★

Ask a group of students who speak the same language to conduct an after-school session for teachers about their language and culture.

Develop a peer buddy programme

'I often use peer buddies to support EAL learners who are new to the school, as they can help to explain school routines and offer friendship at breaks and lunchtimes.'

Not all peers will make suitable buddies for new arrival EAL learners; buddies need to be confident, articulate communicators. While they do not need to be bilingual, sharing a strong first language with a child who is an early user of English can be a tremendous advantage.

Taking it further

The Young Interpreter Scheme® (Idea 98) takes peer buddying to a new level, with online training materials available to skill up a team of students to act as helpers for new arrivals and their families. Find out more here: http://emtas.hias. hants.gov.uk/course/view. php?id=30.

It is a good idea to allocate a 'peer buddy' to any new-arrival EAL learner first starting school. Having a pool of potential buddies who can take turns to be with the new arrival on a regular basis will help ensure that no individual is overburdened. Potential buddies should be self-assured, trusted to model good behaviour and confident English speakers. Peers who share a language with the new learner can act as interpreters or translators, which is particularly important for learners who are new to English.

All buddies should undergo basic training to help them understand the requirements of the role. Buddies can support EAL learners both in and out of lessons in many important ways. They can help explain school routines and act as advocates for the new learner, ensuring they remain safe throughout the day. They can also support the new learner in lessons by clarifying tasks and modelling good use of English across the curriculum.

A well-thought-out programme will benefit everyone. New arrivals will feel supported, while buddies learn from training and the opportunity to take on varied responsibilities. When the support finishes, certificates can be awarded in recognition of buddies' efforts.

Personal diaries and timetables

'Our new EAL students often find it really hard to find their way around the school and work out which lesson they should be at next.'

Large school sites can be daunting places to navigate, especially for those who don't speak the language well. Make sure new EAL learners understand how their timetable works and have a clear map of the site.

Secondary schools often provide a personal diary with a timetable and other school information such as a map, which can be a useful *aide-memoire* for new EAL students. Make sure you plan an orientation lesson in the first few days to explain how the timetable works and take a tour of the school buildings using the map. Then write a brief note to the student's parents to find out if they can read English and sign it so you have established a line of communication. If there is no official school diary, provide new English learners with a good-quality workbook which can be personalised. Workbooks may also contain learning resources provided by the school, a visual timetable and survival vocabulary (Idea 4). Include academic keywords from different subjects, maps of the world and the UK, and a basic history timeline. A set of thumbs-up/horizontal/down or red/amber/green traffic light cards can be useful visual tools for learners to show their level of understanding during class work. Personal diaries or journals can be used in many ways depending on a learner's background and level of literacy in English. All learners will benefit from using it as a notebook in which to record new vocabulary and writing in L1 and English. It can also serve as a communication tool for sending messages between home and school in L1 and English.

Taking it further

More advanced learners can use the workbook as a 'dialogue' journal to have a written conversation with the teacher or other supportive adult about things that are important to them. Less literate learners might start with drawings and simple annotations, and more confident writers might produce extensive prose. Since meaning is more important than grammatical accuracy and spelling in the initial stages of learning a language, it helps if the journal reader avoids correcting anything and responds in a similar informal style.

Using *Google Earth*™ and *Google Maps*™ to orientate new arrivals and teach about locality

'I am constantly amazed at how little some new arrivals know about their new situation.'

Maps are a great way to visually show the relationship between different places in the locality. This idea provides the opportunity to introduce all kinds of vocabulary to a new EAL learner.

EAL learners may be disorientated when they first come to live in the United Kingdom. Adjusting to another culture and a new home, and settling into a new school can be confusing and isolating. Students may be unaware of where the United Kingdom is in relation to their home country, where their locality lies within the UK and even where their present home is in relation to the school.

Google Maps™ and *Google Earth*™ are fantastic tools for showing geographical locality and the relationship between places, distances, directions and points of interest.

This activity works well in a one-on-one or small-group situation.

- Begin by asking where the learner used to live, e.g. 'Bangladesh'.
- Allow *Google Earth*™ to show the revolving world as it zooms down to and then within a country.
- Work with the student to use keywords to refine the area, e.g. 'Sylhet', or use the zoom and tilt tools to find a locality that the learner can recognise. They may be able to identify mountain ranges, rivers, cities and other major features.

- Click on photographs as they appear. This may throw up images of places that the learner recognises, which will generate opportunities for conversation in a natural context.
- Next, allow *Google Earth*™ to return to the United Kingdom, perhaps through other countries that the learner has lived in. Learners who have had complicated journeys may be able to trace their route from home to the United Kingdom and so provide further opportunities for discussion.
- From a distance above the United Kingdom, zoom into the area of the learner's home, pointing out major features and places. It can be very motivating to zoom right down on top of the house the learner currently lives in by using the postcode. Next, zoom out a little to show the learner's home in relation to the school.

Taking it further

Type keywords into the search bar to identify points of interest, e.g. 'college', 'leisure centre', 'park' and 'cinema'. Local places that match the keyword will be displayed on the map, ready for further investigation.

Older new arrivals

'I was the top of my class in Ethiopia, now I feel I know nothing.'

Older EAL learners arriving into Year 9 or above may need additional support to settle in as they can become very frustrated about how much they have to catch up on before GCSEs start.

Taking it further

Read about the education system of the countries of origin so that you can ask pertinent questions about a new student's previous schooling during the admissions interview.

Bonus idea ★

It is good practice to allow older EAL learners to follow a reduced number of GCSE courses and to supplement their exam-based courses with an option support or additional teaching session to allow them to review and revise the work at a slower pace (Idea 93). Generally, ESOL qualifications are not recommended until post-16 as even a low grade in English GCSE is worth more on paper than an entry-level ESOL qualification.

It can be a challenge for a secondary school to admit older students who are not fluent in English, not least because public exams are looming. However, many schools have had very positive outcomes from admitting older EAL learners, including refugees and asylum seekers, as they are often already highly educated and motivated to succeed. In the UK, education is a statutory right, regardless of immigration status. School is the best place for a young person to make friends and settle into a new life. Older new arrivals with limited English may need a lot of additional support to access the curriculum quickly. In addition to a day or two's induction and perhaps some in-class support or small-group teaching, make sure you allocate a well-trained and reliable buddy to older students (Idea 6).

Occasionally, if an older student has had limited schooling, it may be appropriate to put them back a year to give them time to develop oral English before embarking on GCSE courses, but this is not recommended for younger students. See the Joint Council for Qualifications (www.jcq.org.uk) for guidance on special exam arrangements for students with fewer than two years in the UK. The exam results of most EAL students who have joined UK education after the start of Year 10 don't have to be counted in final totals. Reading and writing speed tests may need conducting in order to get the full concessions available. (See Idea 20.)

Assessment, planning and target setting

Part 2

Assessing proficiency with languages other than English

'Knowing that an EAL learner has age-appropriate levels in their first language tells us a lot about their previous schooling and their learning potential.'

While having access to an interpreter/translator will make a first language assessment easier, it is still possible to glean a lot of information without one.

It is useful to know about the full language repertoire of the whole school community. For new EAL learners, an accurate assessment of proficiency in their L1, as well as other influencing languages, will help build a more complete picture of their ability and potential. Information collected should include the following:

- the student's first language, as well as all other languages used
- how long each language has been spoken or studied and when and for what purpose
- proficiency levels in speaking, listening, reading and writing each language.

A rigorous assessment of L1 is best achieved in collaboration with a well-educated adult speaker of the same language, as they should be able to establish whether the learner is functioning at an age-appropriate level. Sometimes it isn't possible to secure the services of a trained bilingual practitioner; it may be necessary to seek help from parents or even older students, although confidentiality must be guaranteed in such cases (Idea 11).

School staff should not be dissuaded from assessing a student's L1 because bilingual support is unavailable at the time. First language assessment without the presence of a fluent speaker might include the following:

Speaking and listening

- Watch an informal conversation between students who share the same first language and look out for fluency, eye contact, body language, child-initiated conversation, etc.
- Ask the student to listen to dialogue such as a podcast or short video and ask simple questions in English about what the child has heard.
- Play a sample of audio from a talking book and ask simple questions in English about what the child has heard.

Reading

- Listen to a learner read from an age-appropriate bilingual text – take note of pace, intonation and self-correction (Idea 49).
- Encourage the student to point as they read so that you can follow along, matching the text to what is being read.
- Where possible, check whether the learner is reading for meaning by asking simple questions in English.

Writing

- Sample a piece of writing about a familiar story, setting or situation; consider overall length, handwriting, punctuation, demarcation and evidence of self-correction.

Taking it further

Hampshire Ethnic Minority and Traveller Achievement Service (EMTAS) have produced a comprehensive eLearning guide to L1 assessment. Using video case studies, the unit details how to conduct an L1 assessment without the involvement of an adult L1 speaker. See http://emtas.hias. hants.gov.uk/course/ view.php?id=19 for more details.

Finding and using bilingual help

'It is impossible to overstate the value of having interpreters to help us connect with parents and understand the background of our new EAL learners.'

Depending on the context and the level of confidentiality required, interpreters can range from formally trained professionals to members of staff and even articulate older students.

Taking it further

When a school has important letters to send out, it may be necessary to pay for a professional translation. It is not fair to expect school-based bilingual staff to do this, unless they have a very good standard of education or specialist qualifications. Good translation takes time, and qualified staff may need additional payment for this too.

Bilingual helpers will usually be peripatetic or school-based staff such as teaching assistants. However, don't underestimate the role that parents and learners themselves can have in supporting interpreting. Sixth form students can often put their own language skills to good use supporting younger students, perhaps as part of a community service accreditation. Conduct an audit of the whole school community to identify who can speak, read and write different languages and with what level of proficiency (Idea 5). Many schools now have overseas qualified staff, so it will not only be the modern languages department who are proficient linguists. Think carefully about who can support with what. An informal chat involves a different level of language proficiency and maturity than a formal assessment, which requires an individual to have good first language proficiency as well as a full understanding of the need to be confidential.

When to use bilingual help:

- It is sometimes necessary to have an interpreter present during an initial parent meeting or interview (Idea 2) to help gather critical background information.

- Arrange to have interpreters available for parents' evenings or academic review days and let the parents know in advance that an interpreter will be available; they will be more likely to attend.
- A formal first language assessment (Idea 10) also requires the services of a skilled interpreter or translator, preferably an independent individual with a solid educational background who can help you gain an unbiased, realistic picture of the varying proficiencies that a learner has in other languages.
- Older students can provide informal support in lessons or be reading buddies where confidentiality is not such an issue.

Interpreting (and translation) needs to be an integral part of a school's support mechanism.

EAL proficiency stages – snapshot assessment

'The EAL proficiency stages are such a useful snapshot for all teachers.'

The use of standard EAL proficiency codes across England and Wales makes it easier for all teachers to plan support and differentiation for EAL learners at different stages.

In 2017, for the first time, the Department for Education required all schools to assign EAL proficiency stages to students who speak another language at home and in the community. This data must now be submitted in the School Census every January.

It is important for schools to give the responsibility for assigning the codes to a teacher, rather than a data manager. In most cases, the English teacher who has most recently taught the student will be able to assign a 'best-fit' code (see below). The stage descriptors are designed for non-specialist, cross-curricular use.

The EAL proficiency data collected should enable schools to plan and make provision for EAL students at different stages of development. Many schools will find that there are more EAL students at the developing competence level (code C) and competent (code D) than in the initial stages of learning English. This may have implications for the recruitment of suitable specialist staff.

The EAL proficiency stages are as follows:

A – New to English
B – Early acquisition
C – Developing competence
D – Competent
E – Fluent

EAL assessment frameworks – developmental assessment

'Salim was silent for several months before he spoke at all. Then his language developed rapidly for a year. I was surprised about the unevenness of it all.'

A new language doesn't usually develop smoothly, so it's important to record small steps of progression across the four language skills – listening, speaking, reading and writing – for the first few years. This can then provide a baseline for target setting.

After a few weeks settling in, an in-depth baseline assessment of language development should be conducted, ideally by an English language specialist, using a comprehensive framework of 'can do' statements rather than a formal test. The process of talking to and observing the new EAL learner doing tasks is the most valuable assessment of all. There is no national, statutory EAL assessment framework in the UK, with authorities using locally-based systems for recording progress.

A good assessment framework should show progress from beginner to fluent across the four language skills, with a focus on reading images as well as traditional reading skills to reflect the multimodal nature of our digital world. It should also consider different rates of progress according to the age of the student and their previous experience of schooling.

Additionally, for secondary-age students, the EAL assessment framework needs to be able to show progress in reading and writing *across* the curriculum rather than just in English lessons. A student who has mastered the skills of writing a good description in a narrative for English may still not be able to write an explanation of a process in science.

Taking it further

To help set meaningful language targets, look at rates of progress. Students from well-educated backgrounds can catch up with their peers in a few years, while those who are new to literacy as well will usually take longer to reach age-related expectations.

Bonus idea ★

Download or buy a detailed EAL Assessment Framework from a reputable academic organisation, such as NASSEA (http://nassea.org.uk/eal-assessment-framework) or the Bell Foundation (https://www.bell-foundation.org.uk/eal-assessment-framework-for-schools-version-1-1).

IDEA 14

EAL or SEND?

'When EAL learners fail to make adequate progress, it can be extremely difficult to unpick whether this is solely related to language or culture or if there may be an additional underlying SEND.'

It's important not to jump to conclusions. Take the time to gather information from as wide a range as possible, including from parents, practitioners and, potentially, health professionals.

Teaching tip

When in doubt, seek advice from trained specialists in this area.

The proportion of EAL learners with a special educational need nationally is similar to that of the English-speaking population. Similarly, the proportion of children with SEND nationally who speak another language at home is similar to the proportion of all students who are EAL learners. According to the 2016 School Census, 14.6% of students in special schools have EAL. Schools may wish to scrutinise their own data to check that there is neither over- nor under-representation.

Experience suggests that when EAL learners are having difficulties at school, attributing such difficulties to an underlying SEND is not usually the most relevant of starting points. In the early months in a new country or school setting, there may be many reasons why progress in learning is slow.

First, consider the other barriers that may prevent an EAL learner from making expected progress in class. Look both within the classroom and outside school. Don't rely on formal tests or screening programmes for SEND, as these are generally standardised on a monolingual population. EAL learners may not be able to demonstrate their true capability in test situations because of linguistic and cultural barriers. Even non-verbal tests have inherent bias or will be unfamiliar to students from many parts of the world. Ensure that learners have been well settled in the school over a period of several weeks before carrying out any 'formal' assessment.

It's important to gather a range of evidence to help inform any decisions either way, such as:

- information from parents or carers about their child's early development and previous educational experience
- observation of learners and their social interaction both in and out of class
- assessment of L1 proficiency (Idea 10)
- analysis of English proficiency and progress over time (Idea 13).

It is quite usual for EAL learners to have an uneven profile of achievement across the curriculum, so collect samples of work or talk to teachers from a range of subject areas.

Take a diagnostic approach, and ask questions about all aspects of a learner's experience. Doing so will allow you to filter out irrelevant information and focus on factors that can't be explained by things like medical issues, interrupted education, language, culture or a traumatic past.

Taking it further

Hampshire Ethnic Minority and Traveller Achievement Service (EMTAS) have an extensive range of EAL eLearning, including a comprehensive unit on distinguishing the difference between SEND and EAL: http://emtas.hias.hants.gov.uk/course/view.php?id=19

See also this information from Norfolk: www.schools.norfolk.gov.uk/view/NCC164400.

Identifying able or high-potential learners

'When Grace arrived in our school she spoke no English, but her maths ability was exceptional.'

Identifying talent and potential in EAL learners is quite easy. They often shine in mathematics or practical subjects and their progress in learning English is rapid.

The representation of EAL and ethnic minority learners as able or talented should be broadly in line with that of the WBRI population. Rapid progress in learning English or another language is one sign of a gifted or talented student. Consider these questions when EAL learners are under-represented on a school high-potential list:

- What might be the implications of an under-representation?
- What criteria do the school use to identify high-potential learners, and are they flexible enough to ensure fair opportunities to identify EAL learners, including those new to English?
- Have you looked at subject setting and banding that may put limits on EAL learners' achievements?
- Can you consider talents in music, sport or art, which are less dependent on language skill?
- What about learners working above age-related expectations in L1?

Learners identified as high-potential may be able to draw down additional support or access specific enrichment activities. Encourage learners to take a GCSE or even A level in the first language, showcase music, dance, fashion and other aspects of the students' own cultures, or offer enterprise opportunities for those who actively contribute to running family businesses.

Have flexible curriculum outcomes

'EAL learners are entitled to access the same curriculum as their peers but often require a different mode of output to demonstrate learning in the early stages of learning English.'

Practitioners must look beyond the expected output of written English. Offering opportunities for students to show their understanding orally and visually will allow teachers to observe progress effectively.

How are learners expected to demonstrate progress and attainment within any specific curriculum area? This is an important question, because every EAL learner is at a different stage in the acquisition of English. Those who are new to English will struggle to demonstrate the full extent of their learning through a predominately mono-modal written outcome.

For beginner EAL learners, listening is the first skill to develop, so look for feedback through facial expression, mime and gesture. It can be useful to employ a traffic light cards system, where green demonstrates full understanding, amber indicates the learner is unsure and red indicates confusion.

It will also be much easier to assess understanding orally in the initial stages. This means subject staff may need to make alternative arrangements when the class are doing formal tests. Where possible, use bilingual peers or staff to help with oral feedback. Allow learners to produce annotations and writing in L1; translation can always be done later. Older students may find it helpful to produce extended writing in L1 first and then paraphrase it orally to a teacher if no translator is available. (See Idea 11 for help with accessing bilingual services.)

Teaching tip

Give lots of praise the first time an EAL learner contributes to a class discussion or group presentation. The content may be straightforward, but just taking part can be quite daunting at first.

Bonus idea ★

Make use of a variety of resources to demonstrate learning. Mini-whiteboards will encourage learners to produce visual feedback about their learning through ticks, words and short phrases, or use pictures and graphic organisers (Idea 34) to convey understanding. It will also prove beneficial to enable students to show learning through digital media such as audio recordings, photographs and short video clips.

Target setting

'Rates of progress for EAL learners need to exceed those for monolingual peers so that they can close the gap.'

School assessment managers should use ambitious progress models for EAL learners who start from a low baseline but make rapid progress as their English fluency develops.

Taking it further

When using assessment manager tools to set whole-cohort targets, you may need to override some of the numerical targets that are automatically produced for students who have no KS2 baseline scores. The pre-set algorithms tend to default to lower expectations, whereas EAL learners who have already had a full primary education will in fact make faster-than-average progress. The Fischer Family Trust Student Explorer is a good tool for this process. (Find out more here: https://fft.org.uk/fft/student-explorer.)

All EAL learners should be working towards both language and curricular targets, regardless of English proficiency. It's important to ensure that targets are appropriate, achievable and challenging and are reviewed on a regular basis. It's also good practice to involve learners in the development and review of their own targets. Appropriate targets need to match the stage of language development of the learner. Some targets may operate globally across the curriculum, while others need to be designed within a more subject-specific context. It is important to consider all the external variables and get a reliable baseline assessment using specialist EAL frameworks (Idea 13) before setting targets.

Compare the following targets: 'Begin to use paragraphs' and 'Begin to demarcate science investigation reports using topic headings'. Subject-specific targets work best when they support a wider global target; this helps to ensure that all teachers take responsibility for 'language aware teaching' within their curriculum area rather than just leaving it to the English or EAL department.

Schools may consider creating individual language plans (ILPs) or profiles for cohorts of EAL learners at different levels of proficiency, based on the can-do statements of the EAL assessment framework in use. This will support all teachers with planning to teach specific aspects of speaking, listening, reading and writing across the curriculum.

Language and literacy demands of the curriculum

'We recommend language and literacy objectives are explicitly taught within each subject to enable all students to be successful. We recognise this is particularly beneficial for our EAL learners.'

While specialist vocabulary objectives are a natural starting point, teachers will also need to consider common language features and text types within different subject disciplines.

EAL learners experience the double challenge of having to learn curriculum content alongside the academic language associated with different subjects and activities. So, it is essential that all teachers consider the specific language demands of their curriculum area and plan their lessons accordingly.

Observing peers in their teaching and watching pre-recorded sessions will enable staff to unravel the particular language needed for EAL learners to access key tasks as well as demonstrate full achievement. In this way, specific language demands can be identified and written into curriculum plans.

The language embedded within any subject or activity inherently involves the use of specialist vocabulary and frequently-used phrases, as well as the more specific functions and features of both oral and written language. Some EAL learners have already mastered many of these subject-specific language conventions in their L1, while others may have significant gaps. But planning to tackle the language demands of the curriculum will benefit not only EAL learners but also their monolingual peers, as everyone needs to learn academic language that goes beyond everyday situations.

Teaching tip

The following headings (adapted from Gibbons, 1991) could be used in a planning frame for analysing language demands within a topic: Curriculum objectives (desired outcomes), Key activities (what will be done by learners), Language functions (techniques required in use of language), Language features (tone, style, voice, figurative language, grammar), Language structures (examples of sentence starters, linking words, etc.) and Academic vocabulary (context-related words).

Taking it further

More information about language demands can be found in an article available from the NALDIC resource web archive here: http://www.naldic.org.uk/Resources/NALDIC/Initial%20Teacher%20Education/Documents/EALLanguagedemands.pdf

Planning using Cummins' framework

'I often advise teachers to use Cummins' framework when planning modules of work for classes with EAL learners.'

Cummins' framework helps teachers structure lessons for EAL learners to work on cognitively challenging tasks with enough support and scaffolding.

Taking it further

To find out more about Cummins' framework, visit: https://ealresources. bell-foundation.org.uk/ eal-specialists/research-1970s-onwards-jim-cummins

Jim Cummins, Professor of Education in Canada, developed the Cummins Matrix, also called the Cummins framework. This is a grid with two axes – one concerned with cognitive challenge and the other with the context for language learning. Context describes the place for learning as well as the other people and supports involved. This produces four quadrants, A–D, where A is cognitively undemanding and context reduced; B is cognitively undemanding and context embedded; C is cognitively demanding and context embedded; and D is cognitively demanding and context reduced.

EAL students who are new to English may be supported by tasks that are in quadrant B in the initial stages, e.g. talking to friends while playing a game, or matching words and pictures in a geography topic. But spending too long on low-level tasks will not lead to rapid progress in either language or subject content learning. The tasks that fall in quadrant C, which are both cognitively challenging and 'context embedded', are going to be the most productive long term.

Quadrant C learning tasks could include:

• A practical science lesson where the EAL learner can hear talk about an experiment while observing it in progress. They can see what it is they need to describe. When they hear new phrases like 'the water is giving off steam' or 'the powder is burning with a green light', they have a context on which to 'hang' new language.

- Reading a paragraph and extracting keywords to label a diagram or complete a graphic organiser (Idea 34).

The intention is that by working within quadrant C, you can provide a rich context for EAL learners in all lessons and can plan for high cognitive challenge. Context can be provided by using visuals, real artefacts and experiences, graphic organisers, peer support and practical activities.

Work in quadrant A is not recommended as it contains low-level, meaningless activities such as copying notes from the board or repeating language drills. Tasks in quadrant D offer no contextual support and include independent learning such as writing an essay or an exam question.

Bonus idea ★

Quadrant C tasks aren't limited to classroom-based subjects. Try asking the students to write a set of instructions to sequence after watching a demonstration of a technique in PE, such as serving in tennis.

Statutory assessment arrangements

'I found it really helpful to use a dictionary in my maths GCSE exam so that I could check a few non-maths words in the question that were unfamiliar.'

The exams officer should ensure that the school has purchased suitable bilingual dictionaries for use in exams and, if necessary, applied for extra time for EAL students.

In secondary education, public exams are taken in Years 11 and 13 in England and Wales, and in S5 and S6 in Scotland. The Joint Council for Qualifications (JCQ) produces downloadable guidance on the regulations. These allow EAL students to use a bilingual dictionary in some exams, but there are strict criteria for their use. It is not possible to use a dictionary at all in certain subjects, most notably English and humanities subjects. You can find more information here: www.jcq.org.uk/exams-office/access-arrangements-and-special-consideration/regulations-and-guidance.

The school's examination officer, often working with the SENDco, will need to gather information about a student's date of arrival in the UK, previous education and literacy levels in English in order to confirm the right for additional time to use the dictionary. This is usually allowed for the first three years in UK education. In some cases, it is also possible to apply for additional assistance such as a scribe or reader for a student with EAL. Applications must be made in good time for the June exams. The bilingual dictionaries used should be one-to-one translations only, with no additional help on word usage. Scanning pens, such as the C-Pen Reader, can also be used in some exams.

Curriculum access

Part 3

How to group EAL learners

'This work is too easy. I have already done this work in my country. I am getting bored.'

EAL learners can be adversely affected if they are inappropriately grouped with 'less able' peers.

Making the right decisions about grouping and setting is essential for all EAL learners to reach their full potential. As a rule, EAL learners should be grouped or set according to their academic *potential* rather than current English proficiency or attainment. A curriculum that matches the cognitive ability of the learner builds upon existing skills, maintains motivation and raises self-esteem. It may be necessary to liaise closely with subject teachers to ensure that the majority of EAL students are not placed in lower sets because of reduced English proficiency. EAL learners benefit from effective use of language across the curriculum being modelled by orally proficient English speakers. Offer EAL learners the opportunity to rehearse their ideas with a supportive peer before answering in front of the class, and pair same-language speakers together at first so beginners can converse and think through ideas in a familiar language. However, sometimes you may want to separate same-language speakers so that they have authentic reasons to speak to peers in English; plus, hearing a two-way conversation between confident English speakers can be of benefit. Be flexible about the physical placement of learners within the room, giving them a clear view of the board and seating them close to the teacher without making them feel isolated or conspicuous.

Activating prior knowledge

'EAL learners don't arrive in our classrooms as "blank slates" and neither are they "language disabled".'

Activating prior learning sends 'explicit messages to children that their ideas are of value and that they have an active role to play in their learning.' (DfES, Unit 2, 2006, p. 10)

Whether UK-born or newly-arrived from abroad, EAL learners have a range of knowledge, skills and experiences influenced by their upbringing and previous schooling. EAL learners might have missed some schooling or had uninterrupted education. They may be unused to group work or technology, or have developed unusual skills that should be recognised and built upon. They may have large gaps in curriculum knowledge but still be ahead in certain subjects. They may only know their L1 or be highly literate in other languages, with understanding of literary devices beyond that of their peers. They may know a lot about different countries, cultures and religious traditions, or be particularly resilient and adaptable because of circumstance.

Linguistically and culturally responsive teaching takes account of the wider experiences of EAL learners so as to enable children to reach their academic potential in the future. Practitioners should have high expectations of all their EAL students, recognising their particular strengths and weaknesses and adapting teaching approaches as needed. Effective questioning and peer discussion can identify natural curriculum starting points, along with a KWL grid to find out what students already know. Use of L1 should be facilitated for new concepts or planning reading and writing tasks (Idea 23), with culturally familiar references established throughout the curriculum.

Teaching tip

Activating prior knowledge is not *just* beneficial for EAL learners. Draw on the diverse range of languages and cultures of EAL students to enrich the learning experience for all students. For some British-born monolingual learners, it might be the first time they have met a child from a different ethnicity or heard another language being openly used in the classroom.

L1 as a tool for learning

'You wouldn't stop a child thinking in their first language, so why stop them talking, reading and writing if it helps them with their learning?'

Children at all stages of learning English can benefit from using their first language to support their learning. Knowing when and how to encourage this requires careful mediation by professionals.

Research has shown that once a student has achieved fluency in two or more languages, it provides a cognitive advantage (e.g. Bialystok, 2009). In later life, being bilingual is believed to protect against degenerative brain conditions such as dementia. It has also been established that concepts developed in the L1 can quickly be transferred to English. Additionally, all children will benefit socially and emotionally from maintaining their mother tongue and keeping in contact with their wider family and community.

Encourage more advanced learners to annotate text in L1 during reading tasks, linking the academic and linguistic knowledge acquired in other situations and helping to internalise new language. Provide all EAL learners with vocabulary notebooks so that they can build up personal bilingual language lists. Learners can also use L1 in writing tasks. Allow students to draft their writing in the more familiar language, enabling them to order their thoughts and write more freely. Through this approach, they will be able to partake in cognitively demanding work, developing subject knowledge alongside their peers. The writing can be translated later, and more advanced EAL learners will begin to make partial translations for themselves.

Bloom's taxonomy

'We find Bloom's taxonomy a very helpful tool for analysing the types of questions we ask our EAL learners. We don't want to limit their ability to communicate by only using closed, yes/no questions.'

Bloom's taxonomy describes higher-order thinking skills such as applying knowledge, analysing and evaluating. Key questions can support EAL learners to extend their spoken language.

As you plan language support for your EAL learners, it can be easy to forget the importance of providing cognitively demanding tasks and opportunities to extend and apply new language in context.

Try reviewing Bloom's revised taxonomy on a regular basis to ensure activities challenge learners to use their higher-order thinking skills alongside lower-level processes such as naming and identifying, and recalling facts and information. With appropriate support, such as supportive questioning from a peer or TA, most EAL learners can reach every level on Bloom's framework.

At times, you will want to plan relatively simple tasks that give learners an immediate sense of achievement, e.g. labelling diagrams or playing vocabulary games. However, you should also design more sophisticated activities, such as asking learners to analyse information or argue a case. As you work your way up the framework, EAL learners will require increased support to access content, participate orally and create written outcomes. Bloom's approaches include questioning that promotes higher-order thinking skills (Idea 37), using graphic organisers (Idea 34), encouraging student use of L1 (Idea 23) for oral and written outputs, and adjusting expectations in terms of outcome (Idea 16).

Taking it further

See the Online Resources for this book for a handy diagram of Bloom's revised taxonomy.

Bonus idea ★

Purchase, or create for yourself, a set of Bloom's taxonomy thinking dice. This resource comprises a set of six differently coloured dice representing the six levels on the Bloom's taxonomy framework. The six faces on each dice represent trigger questions framed at the appropriate level, e.g. the bottom level might be *'What is. . . ',* whereas at the top level it might be *'How many ways can you. . . ?'* The dice can be used in lots of ways to improve thinking and questioning skills.

Practise message abundancy

'Oversimplification of the curriculum is one of the least successful strategies a practitioner can employ for their EAL learners.'

Rather than making work easier, EAL students require explicit teaching that communicates the main message of the lesson in several different ways. Amplification, not simplification, is required.

Teaching tip

Reading tasks can be supported by DARTS (Idea 54). In preparation for writing tasks, it can be useful to encourage learners to partially process information using graphic organisers (Idea 34). Additionally, talk-for-writing approaches enable learners to revisit more formal use of language and concepts – useful activities include oral presentations, hot-seating and Socratic talk (Idea 46).

Taking it further

To find out more about 'message abundancy', look at the work of Gibbons (2006; see References and further reading).

Instead of simplifying tasks for EAL learners, use 'message abundancy' techniques – teaching sequences that present the key messages in a variety of ways. This offers several opportunities for learners to pick up and absorb new language and concepts.

In certain situations, message abundancy may happen naturally, e.g. when giving oral explanations, teachers tend to make the same point several times using gesture or visual clues. During question-and-answer sessions, learners also appreciate how teachers recast their language, correcting mistakes naturally by replacing colloquial terminology with more academic forms, e.g. in a maths lesson, the teacher might recast a sentence using the word 'circumference' when the learner had erroneously used the word 'perimeter' for the outside of a circle.

EAL learners benefit from having several opportunities to access the same curriculum content. A sequence might include the following: watching a short video clip, followed by text marking of written material and, finally, having a paired discussion that draws out the main points. This approach uses listening, reading and speaking to get new content across.

Using bilingual dictionaries

'I know that word in my own language. Using the dictionary means I can use the learning from my own country in my school here.'

When used properly, bilingual dictionaries help students transfer knowledge between languages. However, both teachers and students need to learn how to maximise the use of such materials.

School libraries can acquire a comprehensive range of bilingual dictionaries ready to be loaned to EAL learners when required. If possible, suggest that parents or the school purchase a small portable bilingual dictionary for each child, and encourage them to bring it to school every day. Be aware that print-only bilingual dictionaries will only be useful when learners have well-developed literacy in L1. It is possible, however, to source versions that provide audio support through CD-ROMs and *TalkingPENs*. When looking up English words, you may find that learners who are insecure in sequencing the letters of the English alphabet take an unacceptable length of time to find the right word (Idea 70). For this reason, they may be more comfortable with online dictionaries or translation apps such as *Google Translate*™.

Even learners who can translate between languages do not necessarily know how to make the best use of a dictionary. Ensure learners don't just translate the first matching word they find in the dictionary. Help learners to:

- read through the different contextual sentences to consider each meaning in order to be sure they have the correct word before translation.
- check the part of speech of a word and identify collocations (Idea 75).
- know how to use phonetic spelling to pronounce words.

> **Teaching tip**
>
> For older literate learners, it may be possible to find subject-specific bilingual dictionaries for mathematics and science.

> **Bonus idea**
>
> During writing tasks, some learners construct texts in their head using their L1, and will subsequently make a translation into English before committing the words to paper. Encourage them to look up translations of appropriate words that they know in L1 – this will help learners develop a more varied English vocabulary.

Comprehensible input

'The best situation for learning a second language occurs when teachers provide "comprehensible input" in low-anxiety situations, containing messages that students really want to hear.'

Stephen Krashen has been an influential theorist and researcher in the field of second language acquisition.

Stephen Krashen's *Principles and Practice in Second Language Acquisition* (1982) introduced some key principles of second language learning. The first of these is that learners *acquire* a second language by understanding messages. They will produce their own language when they are ready; it is the teacher's role to provide real communicative and 'comprehensible input', and not force the learner to speak or correct production and pronunciation through exercises or drills.

Krashen highlights the difference between acquisition and learning. In the initial stages of learning, the learner focuses on listening, understanding and making meaning. Krashen believes that after this period of acquisition, a learner starts to self-correct or 'monitor' the language they produce and takes notice of grammar rules, such as adding '-ed' to the past tense in English. For this 'monitoring' to work, more advanced EAL learners need teachers to focus on the structure and forms of the new language.

Another of Krashen's principles is the affective filter, which explains how the learner is affected by external variables such as motivation, self-confidence and anxiety. Krashen claims that learners with high motivation, a good self-image, and a low level of anxiety are better equipped for success in second language acquisition.

The implications of Krashen's work are far-reaching for EAL teaching. Secondary schools need to provide a safe, settled environment from the start, then some general support for curriculum access. But there is also a continued need for specialist language teaching, years after learners have achieved oral fluency, to consolidate their learning.

Here are some top tips for ensuring 'comprehensible input':

- Monitor your own language by giving clear instructions and straightforward explanations, and avoiding colloquial or metaphorical phrases.
- Ensure that the learner feels comfortable in your class with sympathetic peer (or adult) support.

Teachers should also consider EAL students' 'comprehensible output' and make sure that they have opportunities to make oral contributions. Support them with talk prompts or role cards (see Idea 38).

> **Bonus idea** ★
>
> Teachers need to draw attention to grammar features using examples. Don't worry too much about the terminology, but highlight the patterns such as verb forms, comparative sentences and how we modify nouns.

Making the most of translation tools

'Having access to a web-based translation tool can be a real life-saver when a bilingual adult is unavailable.'

Routine access to translation tools is an essential element of any teacher's toolkit. Understanding the strengths and weaknesses of the available technologies will reduce the chances of making embarrassing mistakes.

Teaching tip

Avoid translating anything formal such as letters to parents as this can cause embarrassing mistakes!

Teachers can use translation tools for resource preparation prior to a lesson. However, they will need to ensure they know which language is the student's strongest language (as the child may know several) and, where needed, whether the student is literate enough to read anything written in that L1.

Teachers could prepare concise lesson aims that will give unambiguous translations. They could also prepare dual-language keyword lists, bearing in mind that some words have several synonyms. Web-based translation tools are improving all the time, and moving far beyond simple word-for-word translation. A tool like *Google Translate*™ uses context to pull translation from known quality equivalents around the internet. Consequently, some languages are more accurate than others due to the number of texts available.

Here are a few translation tips and tricks:

- Single words generally translate well, but beware homonyms, e.g. root (scientific and mathematical), root (grammar), roots (idiomatic).
- Remove embedded clauses from paragraphs as this will give more accurate translation.
- Reverse translate to check for accuracy.

- Use tools that enable a user to hear the translation read aloud as some learners cannot read their L1.

New-to-English learners should have access to a range of different technologies during lessons to clarify everyday language as well as more academic terminology. This could be through online translation tools, browser plugins or portable devices and associated apps. Encourage older same-language speakers to talk about translation and make comparisons between languages; this will help learners to notice patterns that make sense to them and allow them to think about structure and purpose in use of language.

Connected portable devices such as tablets and phones have particular resonance for the classroom. Apps can provide instant word- and sentence-level translation of digital text, which is so much quicker than using a paper-based dictionary. Moreover, modern apps now enable two-way bilingual conversations. Using a modern app like *SayHi*, the in-built microphone can 'listen' for speech, render that on-screen, translate the text and output this in a synthesised voice. This avoids the need to type text before translation and enables children who are not fully literate in L1 to benefit as well.

Bonus idea ★

You can use an app like *Google Translate*™ and the camera on your tablet/phone to 'scan' some printed text in one language and translate into a range of other languages. If you install the various language packs, you can even use the technology in situations where there is no internet connection.

Set up technology for L1 use

'Sammi often uses her tablet to read articles and note-take in Polish. This is extremely useful for her geography homework.'

If your bilingual students want to be able to use ICT for learning through L1, then it is important that the technology be set up properly to allow them to interact bi-directionally via voice and text.

Setting computers up for different languages will enable students to use translation tools effectively (Idea 28). They can read their own languages and potentially hear them read aloud in an authentic voice, as well as input text via voice, type their own script using digital writing tools or conduct searches in L1.

You can also enable technology to read aloud text (text-to-speech). This might require the installation of language voice packs or specialised apps, or changing the language/region of the operating system itself (usually relatively simple on a tablet device).

Modern operating systems include full character sets of all the major scripts across the world which need to be set up on a case-by-case basis for text input. Keyboards are relatively easy to set up for other languages; the first place to look is in the *Control Panel* or *Settings* app (for Windows) or *System Preferences* (for Mac). Here you will find the option to change the keyboard set-up to allow other language input. Once installed, you will be able to toggle between keyboards using a shortcut icon or key combination. Set up the soft keyboard on tablet devices via the *Settings* app. You may also want to set up word processors to be able to access the appropriate L1 dictionary to use the error-checking facilities that these provide.

Interactive whiteboards (IWBs) and visualisers

'Once my students are focused towards the whiteboard, I can scan their faces. It gives me immediate feedback on whether they are comprehending my input or not.'

Projecting onto a whiteboard is a great way to help EAL learners focus on a specific item of interest. You can highlight specific content, enlarge resources, deliver multimedia content and model practical or literacy-based learning.

IWBs provide useful functionality for teaching and learning in general, provided they are not simply used for 'chalk and talk'. You can embed subject-specific demonstrations of equipment, such as protractors and compasses in maths.

Visualisers can add another dimension to your teaching, allowing you to make meaning more explicit for EAL learners. They are useful for enlarging small organisms or examining artefacts like hair or a thumbprint. Visualisers are perfect for showing a top-down view of how to do something, e.g. modelling cursive script or demonstrating how to measure distance on a map using a piece of string. It is also possible to perform shared reading, with the additional advantage of being able to show visuals alongside the text.

Visualisers provide an immediate way to show the whole class a piece of work in progress, e.g. group planning in the form of a storyboard or concept map, an incomplete piece of art work or a first draft of a piece of writing, modelling expectations for learners and encouraging peer review. You can also get wireless visualisers, so that you can walk around the room and project work instantly onto the whiteboard.

Bonus idea ★

It's possible to use a tablet as a visualiser using software like *iVisualiser*, available from Apple's *App Store*. You can take a picture with the camera or import an image from the camera roll and then use the in-built tools to annotate over the top of the still image. The app also allows you to annotate over the top of a live video feed from the tablet's camera. It's possible to take a screenshot of whatever annotations have been made in either mode of operation.

Using images and video

'At the beginning, I could not understand a single thing. Only the pictures gave me a clue to what is going on.'

EAL learners at all levels benefit from access to good visuals to support their understanding and enhance learning.

Teaching tip

It's possible to find images on the internet that can be used in educational projects – these have different types of Creative Commons attribution which defines how each image can be used. Use a search facility such as *CC Search* to find them: https://ccsearch. creativecommons.org.

Access to good-quality images, whether printed or digital, is essential for working with EAL learners. It is worth building up a good selection to support subjects across the curriculum; a carefully chosen image will make ideas and concepts much more explicit.

Try developing cognitively demanding tasks for new-to-English learners that are non-verbal and require manipulation of printed or digital images. Encourage learners to:

- Sort or match photographs based on particular criteria, such as a historical time period.
- Use collage as a framework for comparing and contrasting ideas, e.g. settings, characters or themes within stories.
- Rank images on set criteria, such as mathematical scale.
- Develop a visual narrative from a set of images to explain a sequence of events, e.g. a physical, chemical or biological process or the causes of a historical incident or environmental disaster.
- Choose historical visual sources to support a particular point of view.
- Interpret details in one image by overlaying with another, such as when matching a map to a satellite photograph.
- Predict details in obscured parts of an image, e.g. continue a trend in a graph or draw in the missing organisms in a food web.

Images are also excellent for developing oracy and literacy across the curriculum. Projecting images onto the whiteboard at the start of a lesson helps to contextualise work coming up later or to recap content from a previous lesson. Show a close-up of an image and ask the class to theorise about its identity – this is an excellent way to model the use of modal verbs.

Some learners have difficulty with annotating their own work; reviewing each other's work helps reinforce technical language and model language structures that they will need to use in their writing. Annotating images, digitally or in print, also helps develop media literacy. Ask learners to annotate different parts of an image, e.g. an X-ray or ultrasound, a painting or drawing, or an image of war. You can also stimulate creative writing by getting learners to talk and then write about a series of connected book illustrations without the text.

Taking it further

Get learners to talk in depth about one or more images using a website such as the *New York Times' What's Going On in This Picture?* feature (www.nytimes.com/column/learning-whats-going-on-in-this-picture) or images from the NEN Gallery to develop students' critical literacy and inference; this type of work encourages the use of more formal talk to bridge the gap between thinking, talking and writing. They will have to speculate and justify their opinions orally, which is good preparation for analytical writing.

Finding and using internet-based sources

'I usually select suitable websites for my EAL learners as typically they are unable to discriminate appropriate sources for themselves.'

Although some information sources on the internet are designed for younger audiences, most are not. It's counter-productive to offer texts to EAL learners that are neither age-appropriate nor comprehensible.

The internet can be a bewildering place for learners, particularly those still acquiring cognitive academic proficiency in English. Not only are there numerous sources, but the quality, reliability and level of language will all affect the usefulness of the information. For this reason, it is best to prepare a limited list of appropriate websites for each topic or activity. This will help EAL learners who may otherwise waste a lot of time on irrelevant or inaccessible information.

Utilising effective search techniques will help EAL learners because successful searches generally produce a smaller number of search results with a better match to the initial keywords.

Recommended tips and tricks include ensuring that learners limit the number of keywords in searches, don't use high frequency words as part of their searches; check that words are spelled correctly and avoid subject-specific words with double meanings. They should review the number of page results – lower numbers are generally good – and know how to use advanced search techniques. It may be appropriate for older students to use proficiency in L1 to search for and access information in a preferred language, while texts beyond the reach of students can be opened up through text-to-speech.

Bonus idea ★

Research the most useful child-friendly search engines and information sources and ensure they are bookmarked on the school's network. A couple of useful websites include the *Simple English* version of *Wikipedia* (https://simple.wikipedia.org), *Kid Rex* (www.kidrex.org) and *News in Levels* (www.newsinlevels.com).

Viewing and producing infographics

'Infographics are a powerful way to convey information through comprehensible graphics and succinct use of text.'

Infographics are a trendy type of information that can be found everywhere – both in print and on the internet. They are a versatile educational tool. They can be used to provide contextualised information to help learners internalise and repurpose information.

Infographics are a type of key visual with their basis in data. EAL learners may find them helpful for accessing information before a presentation or writing task. You could give students part-completed infographics and ask them to fill in the blank spaces with content prepared by you or generated by themselves.

Students revisit and/or discover additional information as well as create new meanings for themselves through the process of producing their own infographics. The minimal use of text is supportive for most EAL learners, as it helps them to present complex data without the need to produce large quantities of cohesive text.

More ideas include showing EAL learners examples of different types of infographics and how to insert graphs and charts in *Excel*, and inviting them to present their findings. Try tasking learners with explaining a specific issue, e.g. global warming, or illustrating a geological process using maps, flow diagrams and charts, e.g. an earthquake. Encourage learners to create a timeline infographic (e.g. the life of a significant person) or a comparison infographic (e.g. compare and contrast places or events), or to use an infographic to present a weather report or news article.

Teaching tip

Infographics can be sourced from all sorts of different places (remember to check their provenance) – try magazines, newspapers and the internet.

Taking it further

Install software like *Canva* or *Easelly* for easy creation of infographics. This type of software offers easily editable templates and additional graphical assets to create professional-looking infographics. (See www.canva.com and www.easel.ly.)

Bonus idea ★

Use completed infographics as a quick assessment point. Students can also use them as revision guides where appropriate.

IDEA 34

Graphic organisers (and key visuals)

'The most useful support strategies for more advanced learners are graphic organisers as they help with almost all print-based activities.'

A graphic organiser helps EAL learners both extract information from their reading and organise their thoughts to prepare for writing.

Graphic organisers take the form of blank templates that act as a holding area for different types of information. Each type of graphic organiser lends itself to specific language functions and discourse markers. Use them when learners are required to process a lot of information before a formal presentation or piece of writing. This way, learners can move towards higher-order thinking, including explanation, hypothesis and prediction (Idea 24).

Here are some examples of different types of graphic organisers, arranged by the organisational mechanism they can be used to support:

- Sorting – retrieval charts, tree diagrams.
- Sequencing – storyboards, timelines, flow-charts, branching diagrams, cycles.
- Making logical connections – cause-and-effect diagrams, mind maps.
- Comparing and contrasting – tables, Venn diagrams.
- Ordering and ranking – ladders and pyramids
- Concluding and evaluating – living graphs (Idea 55).

To illustrate the use of graphic organisers, consider the following activity. A Year 7 class has been asked to investigate the pros and cons of building a dam at a particular site. They need

> **Teaching tip**
>
> Encourage learners to conduct paired or group work around 'the water cycle' or another key visual. Invite learners to piece together an incomplete version using information drawn from other sources. Incomplete versions would also work well as a barrier game (Idea 42) for a pair of learners.

to collate evidence from a range of sources and use the information to write a discursive text that presents all the arguments. A learner could use a simple table to sort information into two groups – pros and cons. Additionally, he or she might choose a Venn diagram to help organise information into impacts that affect humans, the environment or both.

Having part-processed the information, EAL learners will find the demands of the writing task much easier, because they can simply refer to the table or Venn diagram rather than having to reread the original source material. Staging a task like this really supports EAL learners in more formal oral and written tasks.

Key visuals are information packages that aid understanding by showing the relationships between thinking skills, language structures and graphic organisers. They relate closely to a knowledge framework such as that of Mohan (1986), or a genre taxonomy such as that of Rose and Martin (2012).

Some key visuals are subject-specific, e.g. in science, food webs and pyramids of numbers conceptually show how organisms are connected with each other and their environment. Here, the size and position of visual elements, such as pictures and symbols, imply semantic relationships; together with concise text, they help learners recall new concepts and academic language.

Other key visuals are self-contained narratives that can support the development of explanatory writing. A historical key visual, like a diagram of the triangular slave trade, conveys factual information alongside concepts. Using this type of resource, with appropriate time adverbials, learners can produce an explanation of the cycle of events. The visual helps to develop texts that have a logical structure and cause-and-effect language.

Taking it further

Learners can create their own graphic organisers for revision or note taking. When studying a historical theme, ask learners to produce a timeline to record events sequentially. This will help reinforce the sequence of events and main facts and act as a trigger for information recall.

Maximising use of mobile devices – tablets and phones

'Vladimir has only been here six weeks, but he gave a presentation about the solar system in English by using L1 websites and translators on his tablet to help him.'

Mobile devices have tremendous potential for supporting EAL learners because they promote multimodal learning through clearly rendered text and high-quality audio-visual elements.

While mobile technologies can be ideal personal learning devices, their portability also makes them effective for collaborative learning (Idea 41), as larger tablets can easily be shared within a group-learning situation. The touch-sensitive mode of operation can also support learners who may be unfamiliar with the use of complicated computer operating systems, keyboards and mice. Translation apps (Idea 28) also offer teachers the opportunity to communicate with their students.

Mobile devices all feature eBook reading technology, and finding and managing books and articles (in any language) is easy with apps like *iBooks* and *Kindle*. Some textbooks provide an immersive experience through text, animated images and the ability to listen to professionally recorded narration. Digital texts can also be read aloud using a tablet's in-built text-to-speech synthesis. Users have access to context-sensitive dictionaries and, potentially, translation capability as well.

Mobile devices can be used to support learning across the curriculum, facilitating acquisition of the target language in context and offering beginner EAL learners different ways of demonstrating understanding. Students can use *Wikipedia* in their own language and then

Bonus idea ★

Some EAL learners might benefit from playing around with the various voice assistants incorporated into modern technology, e.g. *Google Assistant, Siri, Cortana* or *Alexa.* These technologies listen out for natural questions and are a quick way to search for answers on mobile devices. Not only do they cut out the need to type accurately but learners will also be able to practise their speech and improve their ability to ask natural questions by judging whether or not the system registers correctly and provides sensible answers.

transfer text to a translation app to be edited and put into a presentation. The camera allows students to integrate images and video into curriculum projects, producing graphic texts (Idea 62) or delivering oral presentations, etc.

Supportive word processors enable students to easily integrate text (in any language), images/ video and sound together in documents as well as providing error-checking tools. Text-to-speech can read back what has been written and speech-to-text can enable a student to enter text quickly via voice rather than typing.

In order to maximise use of mobile devices, ensure that:

- You find a suitable way to connect the device to a data projector through the use of adapters, software or hardware.
- The in-built text-to-speech option is enabled within the device's settings.
- Soft keyboards are set up for the different L1s used by literate EAL learners in the school.
- Dictionary apps like *Dictionary.com* are installed.
- Language-learning apps, such as *Babbel* or *Duolingo,* are also available.
- Two-way translation apps like *SayHi* are readily accessible.

Teaching tip

Check out some suitable apps for secondary age EAL learners here: http://documents.hants. gov.uk/education/ EMTASSecondary PhaseAppWheel.docx

Encouraging speaking and listening

Part 4

Understanding the difference between BICS and CALP

'Sameena has only been here for six months, and she is already speaking fluently!'

New-to-English learners acquire basic, spoken language quickly compared with the language of learning, which takes much longer.

Professor Jim Cummins highlights the difference and continuum between Basic Interpersonal Communication Skill (BICS), the speech of everyday life, and Cognitive Academic Language Proficiency (CALP), the language that we use in school learning.

EAL learners acquire BICS through speaking and listening in everyday situations, supported by context – surroundings, gestures, etc. It generally takes one or two years to acquire BICS and be confident speakers of English in most situations but the development of colloquial language continues throughout life. Older learners may develop spoken fluency very quickly if they have studied English in their country already.

In contrast, CALP is learnt rather than acquired, linked to the thoughts, concepts and processes taught within school and learning. CALP is much more abstract and 'context reduced', found mainly in written texts and with fewer visual supports.

Research in the USA and a few small studies in the UK (e.g. Collier and Thomas, 1997) suggest that CALP often takes seven to ten years to develop, especially when learners do not have secure literacy in L1. Many EAL learners' progress stalls after three or four years when they need additional teaching to support the development of CALP across the curriculum.

Effective questioning techniques

'Sometimes my teacher asks so many questions I have no time to think and I cannot answer what I know.'

All learners benefit from having more thinking time after being asked open-ended questions. EAL learners need this even more so.

A perennial worry for many teachers is the lack of response by EAL learners during teacher-led discussions, especially in whole-class situations. This can be true for both beginners and learners who are developing competence. While recognising that it is important to respect a short 'silent phase' for those new to English, before long such learners should be taking part along with their peers.

Establish a culture that encourages all learners to take risks without the worry of being wrong, and give learners plenty of thinking time prior to asking for a response. Avoid closed questions that require yes/no or single-word answers; use more open-ended questions that require greater detail or have many possible answers – these give learners more opportunity to show what they do and don't know. Employ the use of mini-whiteboards and visual feedback systems, enabling reticent talkers to participate visually at first, and encouraging more oral contribution in the future. Initiate a 'no hands up' rule, allowing you to control who attempts to answer questions, and encourage learners to discuss the question in pairs or groups of three, providing an opportunity to rehearse answers. Where individuals and groups need to report back in turn, allow beginners to take their turn later in the sequence so that they can hear answers being modelled by their peers.

Teaching tip

Take a look at Marion Blank's four levels of questions in order to find out how to make questioning more effective and formalised throughout the whole school. There are many free resources on the internet that have been adapted from Blank's ideas.

Bonus idea ★

Share a grid of key questions related to Bloom's taxonomy (Idea 24), with the additional adults that support EAL learners helping them choose their language and thereby extend students' spoken answers.

Speaking frames

'It's sometimes really hard for the EAL learners to get started in a discussion because the other students in my class are so talkative.'

Having a speaking frame available to support newer EAL learners can be a help in many subject lessons.

It is well established that most EAL learners need additional support for certain kinds of writing – perhaps sentence starters or writing frames (Idea 61). However, it is also true that some new arrivals who are reticent speakers will benefit from having some scaffolding to support their speaking as well. Learners may find it helpful to have lesson-specific talking prompts, particularly in more formal situations such as debates, group discussions or evaluative responses. Speaking frames, or talk prompts, are designed to encourage learners to participate in a range of different oral contexts.

Some learners will be able to read and use simple questions, whereas others may require a more detailed script to give them practice with key oral interactions such as borrowing a book from the library or getting ready for PE.

At their simplest, talking prompts can be open-ended sentence starters and commonly used phrases designed to prompt colloquial language needed for everyday activities, e.g. when ordering lunch, *'What sandwiches have you got?', 'I'd like the. . .' or 'I need to put some money on my card'*. Curriculum-related talking frames aim to scaffold the development of more extended or presentational language. They tend to include more sophisticated sentence structures and conjunctions and may include key vocabulary, e.g. in for-and-against arguments, *'I think that. . .', 'I agree/disagree with. . . because. . .', 'Other reasons include. . .', 'Also/additionally. . .' or 'To conclude. . .'*.

Defining and assigning group roles

'I didn't like running group problem-solving activities in maths lessons until the EAL teacher showed me how to organise the groups effectively.'

EAL learners often benefit from participating in structured group tasks with clearly defined roles.

Teenage EAL learners may often be reluctant to work with their peers in groups, even though they can understand the gist of the lesson. Adolescent shyness may prevent some students from talking at all in class and a teacher may need to work hard to include them in discussions and group activities.

Engineer student working groups carefully, and assign the reluctant or beginner EAL learner to a small but essential role, such as timekeeper, so that they can begin to join in without pressure to contribute. Another idea is to create specific group role cards so that the student has an idea of what to do and say before the group starts on a task.

- Chair – organise the group and make sure everyone understands what to do.
- Clarifier – check the understanding of other group members.
- Recorder/Explainer – write down the methods used and be ready to explain and demonstrate to the class.
- Reporter – record key vocabulary and make sure everyone stays on task.

More competent EAL students could be made Clarifier, which gives them permission to ask questions about things they do not understand. The most advanced learners will be able to take on Chair or Reporter roles with the expectations clarified.

Teaching tip

Do not expect new EAL learners to talk much at first. They will gain a lot from listening to others during group work and gradually take on more responsibility as their confidence increases.

Pronunciation and intonation

'Xiang was really reluctant to speak in class because he thought other students would laugh at his pronunciation.'

Sometimes a teacher will need to give specific one-to-one support to an EAL student to help them learn and practise difficult sounds in spoken English.

Taking it further

Show students how to access an online course such as the BBC's *Sounds of English* (www.bbc. co.uk/learningenglish/ english/features/ pronunciation) or *One Stop English* (www. onestopenglish.com/ skills/pronunciation).

Younger children learning a second language pick up the sounds very quickly, often through play-rhyming, singing and imitating everyone around them. In secondary schools, achieving spoken fluency can be much more difficult because the learning environment is more focused on the written word.

Older, new-to-English students may be very self-conscious about their pronunciation in English. They will want to sound as much like their peers as possible and may need additional help with pronunciation practice. This support needs to be given subtly, and not in a public space, as accent and vocal tone is a very personal thing.

Each learner brings his or her own issues when pronouncing English, but the most common difficulties are related to sounds in the first language. Sounds that are likely to prove more difficult to most EAL learners include:

1 Vowels – English has more vowel sounds than many other languages, but in speech the medial vowels are often unstressed (see next page) so you do not hear them clearly.
2 'Th' (in both voiced 'the' and unvoiced 'thing' forms).
3 Dark 'l' as in 'full'.
4 Silent letters (knee, folk, often).

Intonation

Word stress and intonation are very important in English. We can change the meaning of a sentence just by altering the stressed syllable. Consider these examples:

I don't want to go to school. . . (but maybe you do)

I don't want to go to **school**. . . (but I do want to go somewhere else)

When a vowel is unstressed it sounds like 'uh'. EAL learners should be encouraged to notice how this sounds in normal speech. Words like act**or**, bak**er** and pict**ure** all have an unstressed vowel at the end. One reason why it is so hard to spell English is that in speech we hear the unstressed vowel sound but we do not know which letter is used to represent it.

Bonus idea ★

Produce two lists of minimal pairs (fan/van; off/of; fine/vine; safe/save). Read a word from either list at random and ask students to tick them when heard. Then see if they can choose the right word to complete a sentence, e.g. She bought a new *fan/van*.

On collaboration

'I usually group my developing EAL learners with more confident peers.'

Building on Vygotsky's theory of the Zone of Proximal Development (ZPD), well-constructed and collaborative tasks enable an EAL learner to perform at a higher level when supported by a linguistically more capable peer.

Teaching tip

With students, develop a set of agreed ground rules for collaboration and exploratory talk. Make these available as work cards and/or stick them on a prominent wall in each classroom.

The distinctive position for learning EAL is that students acquire language best through the context of the curriculum. Equally important is the notion that talking, especially exploratory talk, where young people construct new ideas and meanings through peer-talk, enables EAL learners to experiment with curriculum-based language in a supportive, non-threatening environment first. Because knowledge is being shared between participants, there is plenty of opportunity for active listening, paraphrasing, recasting and repetition.

However, it's important to recognise that effective collaboration does not necessarily occur just because students are working in pairs or small groups. To make group work genuinely collaborative and to create thinking together classrooms, teachers should:

- Take an active role in guiding their students' use of language and modelling expectations for them.
- Establish specific student roles within working groups (Idea 39).
- Negotiate a set of ground rules about exploratory talk with their students.
- Devise activities that promote shared knowledge, encourage debate and facilitate joint reasoning.

In some schools, the overall ethos may be a barrier to collaborative talk-based learning. In other cases, the EAL learners themselves will not be familiar with talk-based learning because of the school cultures in their own country. Teachers may have to experiment gradually with collaborative activities.

Collaborative, friendly approaches encourage students to think and work together within information-sharing contexts. They might involve processing activities like matching, sorting and ranking information. They may also include information gap activities, such as barrier games (Idea 42) and Dictogloss (Idea 64).

Find out more about thinking together approaches from *Thinking Together at Key Stage 3* (http://thinkingtogether.educ. cam.ac.uk/projects/keystage3) and look at the resources produced by Voice 21 (www.voice21.org).

Barrier games

'Information gap tasks or barrier games are great for Friday afternoons when we're all tired. I read out instructions and the students try to complete a diagram.'

Listening to carefully worded instructions to complete a picture or completing a sheet with partial information provides realistic language models for all learners, including EAL students.

This talk-based strategy is good for young people at a beginner or intermediate stage of learning English. Information gap tasks (barrier games) support the development of realistic speaking and listening skills. Barrier games can also help to develop instructional language, use of present tense, negotiating and questioning language, comparative terms, descriptive terminology and subject-specific language.

Typically, in an information gap session, learners are paired, and each participant has a different piece of information, maybe a drawing or a text with some elements omitted. During the session, participants sit back to back or on either side of a physical barrier to prevent them from seeing what the other possesses. Ensure they can communicate easily, both orally and through non-verbal cues. One participant provides a detailed description of a 'resource' that they have been given or made themselves, and the other participant must recreate it as accurately as possible.

Sometimes the pair must read out some text and work out differences in their information. Resources can be selected from any subject; they function best when linked to work currently occurring in the mainstream curriculum.

Sometimes, a pair of learners work together to complete a resource from two different versions that they both possess. As each learner holds information that the other needs, they must work collaboratively to piece together a complete version. Each learner takes turns to ask questions to obtain information missing on their resource, e.g. *What is next to. . . ? What colour is. . . ? Is it larger than. . . ? How many. . . ?* Questions tend to focus on visual details such as size, position, shape, colour and amount, and written information such as text and numbers.

The resources should be similar to each other but with a number of significant omissions. Obviously, every omission on one resource must be visible on the other. Visual resources that work well for this type of activity include maps, diagrams, graphs, paintings, tables of information and timelines.

Bonus idea ★

Try making a problem-solving information gap task, such as providing two different texts with information about a scientist and a single set of questions for the pair to answer collaboratively.

IDEA 43

Use of audio

'I can get more meaning if the words are read aloud to me.'

As they progress through the initial stages of acquiring English, many EAL learners hear and understand better than they read and write. Presenting a key text or other information orally is a simple way to open up access to the curriculum.

Taking it further

Check out the Audio Network, which has a large curated set of free-to-use audio files for educational purposes (www.nen.gov.uk/learning-resources/audio-network).

Providing learners with oral access to key texts makes meaning more explicit for EAL learners. Oral versions of books and poems can often be found on CDs, and audio books can be listened to on eBook readers. Digital texts can be read aloud from a computer or mobile device via text-to-speech technology in real-time (Idea 35).

Find audio files or podcasts that demonstrate particular aspects of language use across the curriculum. You could play famous speeches to demonstrate use of formal, standard English. Radio plays or shows might be useful for modelling more informal talk and highlighting the differences in regional accents. A quick search on the internet can reveal a multitude of podcasts for reinforcing curricular learning. There are also podcasts that focus more on the conversational language required for different everyday contexts.

Bonus idea ★

Don't forget how powerful music is for conveying meaning; a suitable sample of music could be useful for reinforcing metre and mood in a particular poem.

Songs can be useful for consolidating what learners already know; they lend themselves naturally to listening tasks. Get learners listening to songs like *Dem Bones* or *The Elements* and ask them to identify key scientific vocabulary. Certain songs are perfect for demonstrating particular grammatical features, and printed lyrics alongside the recording can be used for active listening and associated reading activities such as text marking and reconstruction exercises.

64

Opinion lines and washing lines

'Opinion line debating is an excellent way to help students prepare for argumentative writing. The emphasis on academic talk has particular resonance for more advanced EAL learners.'

The open-ended nature of these activities encourages students to experiment with language and take more risks as they seek to justify their chosen position along a continuum. The quality and quantity of academic talk successfully models the process and usually converts into better writing.

A simple version of the technique requires you to pose a question or statement that is likely to promote a range of views in the class. In small groups, encourage learners to come to a consensus about where to place the question or statement along an opinion line continuum (from 'strongly agree' to 'strongly disagree').

Once positioned, ask someone from one group to indicate where they placed it along the opinion line and justify their decision. Encourage the rest of the class to offer further evidence or counter-arguments where appropriate. Modelling and talk prompt sheets (Idea 38) can help with scaffolding oral contributions.

In a suitable room, you might like to run the activity more kinaesthetically, first posing one or more questions or statements. Place five large opinion signs along one of the walls, and ask a representative from each group to stand in the appropriate position. Next, ask each representative to justify the chosen position, and allow the rest of the class to support or counter-argue where necessary. If the group members change their mind following the class discussion, then the representative can move to a new position.

> **Teaching tip**
>
> This activity also works well with multiple statements around a theme. Allocate each group a different statement or allow them to choose their own.

> **Bonus idea** ★
>
> **Washing lines provide a way for students to extend their vocabulary by organising language items between extremes, e.g. by ranking words in order of size or scale (big, large, enormous, gigantic, huge, massive, humungous, outsize, immense) or by sorting phrases in order of certainty (definite – certain – probable – likely – fifty-fifty – improbable – unlikely – impossible).**

Quizzing and voting tools

'I don't like to put my hand up in class. I don't want to look stupid.'

A class vote is one way that EAL learners can participate on an equal footing with non-EAL peers.

A quick quiz/vote provides a simple formative assessment opportunity. It enables students to participate in quizzes and class discussions/debates without the need for a significant oral contribution. Physically, they are easy enough to set up using laminated cards. Agree/disagree votes could use thumbs-up/thumbs-down or ticks/crosses; multiple-choice quizzes and opinion lines (Idea 44) could use cards labelled with numbers or letters.

Quizzing/voting apps enable learners to give opinions or answer questions more anonymously so it is not apparent to peers what 'answer' has been provided. However, with many quizzing/voting tools it is also possible to set up the app so that the practitioner knows how each student has responded.

Digital quizzing/voting tools work in different ways – some require access to a computer or mobile device, while others use the camera on a portable device and voting cards, each of which contain a unique code.

Here are a few free digital tools:

1 *Answer Garden* (https://answergarden.ch)

This is a website and associated app that collates typed responses visually in a word cluster for the whole class to view on the IWB. In reply to a question set up by the class teacher, students can either provide a free-form answer or choose from a list of suggestions. An interesting feature of this tool is that each identical vote increases its size on the screen so it is possible to see which responses are the most popular.

2 *Plickers* (https://www.plickers.com)

This is an app that uses the camera on a mobile device to record a student's response made by holding up a card containing a unique code. It does not require a live connection to the internet to work. The teacher can set up a true/false activity as well as a four-answer multiple-choice question.

3 *Socrative* (https://www.socrative.com)

This is a website and two associated apps – one for the teacher and one for the student. The tool provides similar functionality to *Plickers* but requires a wireless internet connection and access to multiple connection points via computers or mobile devices. The practitioner sets up a poll via the website or the teacher app, and students respond via their own dedicated app.

Socratic talk – talk as a tool for thinking

'I like to use able, fluent speakers to observe and critique the way their peers handle group work and oral contributions.'

By organising a Socratic seminar, teachers can extend the quality and extent of exploratory talk across a whole class.

Teaching tip

You will need to do some explicit modelling the first time you try this technique. Also, make sure you use some confident and fluent speakers in the inner circle to get the discussion moving from the start.

A Socratic seminar is a good method for improving oral contributions to a class discussion or debate. The aim is to have two groups of students in the classroom – an inner circle, who discuss an issue, and an outer circle, who listen, observe and feed back on specific linguistic or subject content features (which have been pre-planned by the teacher). EAL learners seated in the outer circle will hear good models of language in discussion and have a chance to listen with a clear purpose to a particular talk technique. More advanced learners can sit in the inner circle (with articulate non-EAL learners) and receive supportive feedback on improving their oracy.

For example, if a class has been reading a poem and learning about the features of poetic language, observers could be asked to record how often a student referred directly to a poetic technique or to the emotive effect of a word. In a debate in PSHE on a controversial topic, a student in the outer circle might be asked to observe how the inner circle students take turns in conversation, or include other members of the group. Example questions include: What are the students doing to show they are listening? What phrases did student use to introduce new ideas? How did students expand on an idea to make it clear? What examples of building on or challenging others' points did you hear?

Follow me starters

'I love running a follow me game at the beginning of the lesson as it helps me assess how well students have recalled previous work and includes everyone in the class.'

'Follow me' is a card-based oral activity that is good for learners who are new to English, as the activity has a simple script from which to work and can be easily differentiated.

In a 'follow me' or 'loop' game, each learner is given one card with both a question and an answer on it. The idea is that one learner starts by reading out the card, which might say something such as 'I am a square, how many lines of symmetry do I have?'. In this case, the learner with the card that says 'I have four; tell me another shape with four right angles' should read it out, and so on. Each card should have only one possible following card to avoid any confusion.

Teachers can find samples easily online, or design their own subject-specific versions. Here is one used for revision of fractions suitable for KS3 maths:

I am 50	I am 6	I am 4	I am 10
You are half of 12	You are a quarter of 16	You are a third of 30	You are a fifth of 25
I am 5	I am 2	I am 12	I am 25
You are a sixth of 12	You are half of 24	You are a quarter of 100	You are a third of 90
I am 30	I am 7	I am 40	I am 33
You are a tenth of 70	You are a fifth of 200	You are a third of 99	You are an eighth of 64
I am 8	I am 75	I am 20	I am 60
You are three quarters of 100	You are two thirds of 30	You are three fifths of 100	You are a third of 150

Reading and viewing

Part 5

Multimodal texts

'My science textbook is really hard to understand. There are so many pictures and diagrams; I don't know which parts are important.'

Most school textbooks and online reading include data, pictures and other visuals, which also need to be 'read' and interpreted.

Multimodal literacy, first proposed by Professors Gunter Kress and Carey Jewitt, involves understanding the diverse ways we have of making meaning, including the written word, spoken language, gesture and images. These are our semiotic resources and can be found in a variety of media.

It can be difficult for learners from cultures where visual imagery is not commonly used in education to understand how we interpret multimodal texts such as advertisements, posters and websites.

Practitioners need to make explicit:

- How bold/italicised fonts, underlining and colour add to the meanings created by the written word.
- How information texts lay out content via titles, topic sentences and paragraphs and how this can be useful to extract meaning.
- Where captions or explanations for key visuals or photographic sources tend to appear (to the left or below) in comparison to titles for tabulated data and graphs (above).
- How information such as asterisks or footnote numbers can be signposted via superscript.
- The meaning of digital writing cues such as red underlining in word-processed documents.
- Specific interpretation of unusual infographics or graphical data in subject lessons.

Use of bilingual texts

'Omar's eyes lit up when we found him a story which was written in both Farsi and English. He immediately started to read in his own language.'

Older EAL learners are likely to be fluent readers in their own language and can use this skill as a rapid way into learning English.

As most older EAL learners and their parents are already literate in their own language, using bilingual texts can have a significant role to play in activating a learner's prior knowledge, as well as supporting their access to the curriculum.

For beginners, a bilingual story provides instant access that can inform subsequent literacy tasks, whether in English or another language. More advanced bilingual learners will benefit from exposure to both texts at the same time. It is quite easy to find translations of Shakespeare and other classic texts that can be used in English lessons (Idea 76).

All learners, including monolingual English speakers, will benefit from being able to see two different scripts on the same page. Get groups to compare specific elements such as text directionality, word breaks and punctuation, and ask them to identify root words that may be common to the two languages.

With younger learners or those whose L1 literacy is not secure, get the family involved. Buy some bilingual story books or eBooks from a reputable company such as MantraLingua (http://uk.mantralingua.com). Free printed bilingual texts can also be accessed from the International Children's Digital Library (ICDL) (http://en.childrenslibrary.org).

Teaching tip

Sometimes, try covering one of the texts or a few words or phrases for more active reading. In this way, bilingual learners will be able to transfer knowledge over from L1 to English and vice versa.

Bonus idea ★

Develop guidance for parents about how to share a book with their child and translate it into the main community languages. Helpful guidance for engaging parents can be obtained from the publication entitled 'Developing reading skills through home languages' (http://www.rnlcom.com/wp-content/uploads/2015/02/Developing-reading-skills-through-home-languages.pdf). A list of bilingual book publishers can be found here: www.uel.ac.uk/schools/cass/research/dual-language-books/publishers.

Choosing appropriate texts

'Some of the books my teachers give me are really difficult for me to understand. The history textbook is so hard for me.'

Even advanced EAL learners can struggle with readability in subject lessons. Students who do not know one word in ten will struggle with comprehension.

Choosing appropriate reading material for EAL learners can be challenging. Many teachers tend to choose books that are too simple or intended for a younger age range, thinking that this will help them understand better. It is also easy to choose texts (particularly non-fiction) that are too demanding for the age and cognitive ability of the EAL learner.

Ensure that recommended texts are well produced with clear fonts and well-chosen illustrations that add contextual meaning. Stories with strong narratives or familiar non-fiction topics will be more appealing than texts without an authentic purpose. Similarly, learners are more likely to engage with texts that relate to their own experiences, reflect the society in which they live and deal with issues of culture and religion sensitively, challenging bias and stereotype where necessary.

For early-stage EAL learners, try to select books that are written with an active voice – this will be more accessible as the learners will mostly be drawing on their experiences in spoken language. Avoid texts that have a lot of colloquial language, as this will lie outside the experience of many new-to-English learners. Where non-fiction texts contain academic and technical language, choose those that provide vocabulary explanations or have glossaries in the back. Make sure that the diagrams and illustrations enhance the meaning rather than add too much additional content.

Taking it further

Plenty of accessible online tools can help calculate readability or approximate grade levels for reading, e.g. www.thewriter.com/what-we-think/readability-checker. These formulae mostly rely on average sentence length and average word length in syllables, as well as other factors such as number of personal pronouns and passive verb forms. One of the most commonly used readability formulae is the Flesch-Kincaid, which correlates closely with reading test comprehension scores.

Bonus idea ★

Older and more advanced EAL readers will be able to access more complex texts through being given graded readers (Idea 52). See also the MESH guide for further ideas: www.meshguides.org/guides/node/112?n=125.

Reading miscue analysis (also called running record)

'When I sat down and spent 30 minutes listening to Pavel reading, I realised that he had all the relevant strategies in place.'

EAL learners may get low reading age scores in tests because of limited vocabulary rather than their inability to decode fluently.

Early acquisition (B) and some developing competence (C) EAL learners (see Idea 12) are often found to have reading ages that are lower than chronological age, as assessed through a standardised reading test. However, these tests can be highly unreliable because of differences in wider cultural understanding.

Miscue analysis is a systematic technique for recording a reader's strengths, supporting the teacher to choose books at the appropriate levels and set appropriate targets.

1 Ask the learner to pick a reading book they think they can read quite well. Photocopy a couple of pages so you also have a copy.
2 Give them time to read through a page silently first, before reading aloud.
3 While the student is reading, tick every correct word, writing the 'miscues' over any mistakes.
4 You need to use an agreed set of codes for miscues, e.g. SC for 'self-correction'. There are many for these codes templates available online.
5 At the end of the session, add up the mistakes in the different categories to give you a clear learning target. A student may make lots of mistakes pronouncing medial vowels, perhaps, or constantly guess the words they cannot read, but get the right grammatical form.

Teaching tip

You can download sample miscue analysis forms and sample texts from various websites. You will need to allow up to an hour per student to complete the process properly, but the in-depth analysis achieved will cut down on unsuitable interventions.

Bonus idea ★

For readers who are not fully fluent, it can be helpful to listen to them in L1 first to gauge fluency and confidence before assessing decoding and self-correction ability in English.

Graded readers (from EFL/ESOL)

'My class were reading *Of Mice and Men*, but I found the funny language difficult to follow. I could hardly understand anything Lennie said.'

Graded readers give more advanced EAL learners an opportunity to access classic texts such as *Dr Jekyll and Mr Hyde*, which might otherwise be impossible to read.

Taking it further

There are also non-fiction graded readers related to curriculum subjects, such as science and geography, and others that are film tie-ins or celebrity biographies.

Bonus idea ★

Ask your fluent and able English speakers to produce abridged versions or chapter summaries of class texts for the EAL students in the class. The craft of summarising will extend their own skills, while supporting the EAL students.

Older EAL readers who have moved beyond the initial stages of reading in English can make rapid progress in fluency and vocabulary learning by reading graded readers. These are produced by many of the larger publishers and are available at various levels from beginner to advanced. The books have a fixed vocabulary level and simplified grammar at lower levels. Many series are also accompanied by a downloadable app or online placement test so that teachers and learners can find the right level.

Graded readers have mainly been written for an EFL audience, so you may find some of the titles at the lower levels cover topics more suitable to tourists or casual visitors to the UK, such as 'visiting London' or 'my holiday in Scotland'. But many of the more advanced titles are abridged versions of classic texts like *A Christmas Carol* or *Pride and Prejudice*, which may be taught as part of an English Literature GCSE course.

Young people who are struggling to manage the sheer amount of reading in English required in Years 10 and 11 will find it very supportive to read the abridged version first to establish the gist of the story and the main characters and setting. Then they can go on to read the original version when they are ready.

Graphic readers/comics

'Before I came to England, I never went to school in my country. I learnt my A, B, C, but there were no books in my house.'

EAL learners who have arrived from countries where there is no universal primary education may need lots of visual support to start reading.

At the initial stages of reading, it is important to find books for EAL learners where the level of language is not too easy but the content is still engaging and culturally suitable for the age and maturity of the learner. Graphic readers present fiction and non-fiction through a more visual, cartoon style than traditional books do, with more informal text, supported visually through stylistic conventions and images that convey meaning. Many also contain graded vocabulary and grammar activities linked to the text.

Some EAL learners may be unfamiliar with cartoons such as Manga, so explain some of the more immediate conventions, e.g. reading directionality and how text is organised to imply narrative, with thoughts and speech bubbles.

For developing active reading of comics, try:

- Text marking – identify time adverbials, setting description, powerful verbs and so on.
- Cloze procedure – blank out individual words that need to be predicted.
- Text reconstruction – remove chunks of text from narrative panes, or speech or thought bubbles, and ask learners to rewrite small sections using their own words.
- Story sequence – provide a scrambled set of panes that require sequencing to retell the story.
- Comic jigsaw – separate all the text from the images and ask learners to recombine them.

Teaching tip

Visual cues can also be confusing. You could prepare learners by asking them to think of ways to visually communicate ideas such as speed, an unpleasant smell or heat without any words.

Taking it further

Buy some graphic readers that relate to specific areas for the curriculum such as *Graphic Shakespeare* (www.salariya.com/books/graphic-shakespeare). Many of these are also rated within the *Accelerated Reader* reading management programme.

DARTs

'In technology lessons, my teachers told us to read the book and complete a table of information about the uses of different tools. Then it was easy to use for revision.'

Transforming text to a new format, including a diagram or chart, helps EAL learners to process and organise new information without the need to understand every word.

Directed Activities Related to Texts (DARTs) are active reading strategies designed to make learners think about and process new concepts while reading. Some DARTs help learners consider the overall structure of a text, while others focus on supporting understanding and interpretation. Choosing the right activity to meet the learning needs of the EAL learners is critical. DARTs can be used effectively across the curriculum with fiction and non-fiction texts.

Reconstructing texts

Some DARTs need teacher preparation in advance. These strategies include cloze (a strategic gap fill), matching sentence halves, sequencing sentences and information-transfer tasks. All of these benefit EAL learners as they require a close reading of the text. Learners need to look carefully for keywords and logical conjunctions to complete or recreate the text.

Analysing texts

Other DARTS are analytical, such as highlighting specific text features, identifying the main idea or topic sentence, adding subheadings or labelling paragraphs. The teacher still needs to read through a text in advance to decide the appropriate strategy. When working with texts from various sources, marking words or phrases in different colours can help organise ideas and language conceptually prior to repurposing text into a different format.

For non-fiction texts such as reports, ask learners to break up an unformatted piece of text using topic sentences and headings or sub-headings that have been provided.

Another strategy is to ask learners to mark important words in preparation for further tasks, e.g. highlighting generic verbs, such as get, put, make, said, to identify where to use more powerful ones.

EAL learners sometimes struggle to signpost their writing effectively using conjunctions and adverbial phrases. In argumentative writing, encourage learners to highlight all the logical conjunctions and mark where additional points are being made as opposed to making counter-arguments.

Bonus idea ★

Once text is categorised, provide learners with graphic organisers (Idea 34). This will help them to part-process chunks of language before transforming it into a new text, e.g. a scientific report, newspaper article or advertisement.

Reading data – living graphs

'My students aren't confident readers of graphical information, nor do they find it easy to link text and data in one paragraph.'

New EAL learners, especially those from other education systems, may need additional support to understand the range of graphical data we use across the curriculum.

Taking it further

Once the position of the pre-written statements has been agreed, learners can sequence them and expand the notes to form a detailed, cohesive piece of writing, e.g. an explanation of how the flow of traffic changes throughout the day.

Analysing and evaluating data is a form of higher-order thinking that is difficult for some EAL learners to fully express through writing. An explanatory text often requires abstract and condensed language and a specific structure and uses cause-and-effect language and a range of technical vocabulary according to the subject area.

Use 'living graphs' to help learners interpret trends and patterns in data that have been obtained through their own investigations, or use graphs drawn from pre-existing data. Living graphs require learners to justify the position of information against a timeline of events.

In preparation, create a variety of true statements that help to describe and explain the overall shape of the graph. Try to include ambiguous or irrelevant information, as this encourages active reading. Produce a set of cards containing all the statements, and ask learners to place them on appropriate positions on the graph if they are true. Encourage the group to discard any irrelevant statements. See the Online Resources for an example of this activity.

Living graphs can be developed around any kind of continuous data, such as the volume of traffic varying over the course of a day, earth movements before, during and after an earthquake or the interrelationship between a predator and its prey over time.

Using technology to support reading

'Hearing a text read aloud enhances understanding and can also help develop reading skills.'

Most EAL learners demonstrate greater proficiency with spoken English than they do with reading and writing. Digital devices and integrated software can read text aloud, enabling learners to access written information that would otherwise be inaccessible to them.

Use of audio books

Where possible, provide learners with aural access to key texts to make meaning more explicit. Audio versions of books and poems can often be found on CDs or in apps, and digital books can be listened to on eBook readers. Set up screen-reading software (see below) on computers so that learners can listen to digital texts.

Websites such as LibriVox (https://librivox.org) now offer free audiobooks of out-of-copyright texts. These vary in quality, so teachers should listen first before recommending individual titles, but it is possible to find most of the English literature set texts in English and other European languages.

Rendering text-to-speech

Screen-reading software, which can be used to read text aloud to a user, enables learners to access written information that would otherwise be inaccessible to them. Some versions work within word processors and web browsers, while others allow text to be pasted from the clipboard. There are also portable versions that need no installation and can be accessed directly from a memory stick. It is also worth having screen readers installed on a laptop or tablet that can be used around the school.

Teaching tip

With software, experiment by choosing appropriate voices and other settings. Some screen readers allow a user to change the speed of oral reading, which can assist learners with differing linguistic and cognitive abilities. It may also be possible to set up the software to highlight text as it is read aloud, helping to reinforce word recognition.

Taking it further

The Balance has a list of different sites for audio books (www.thebalance.com/free-audio-books-the-15-best-sources-online-1357952). You can also use the National Education Network audio section (https://audionetwork.lgfl.org.uk).

Note-taking

'We usually model note-taking in the first few lessons for Year 12 so that all students understand what is expected.'

EAL learners may be slower making notes from textbooks, and even fluent speakers can find listening for main ideas difficult the first few times they do it.

The process of note-taking in a second language is no different from note-taking in L1, so many older EAL learners will know what to do, especially if they are encouraged to write notes in their first language. Obviously, even competent EAL learners will take longer to make notes from extended reading than monolingual speakers, and it is a good idea to give them reading passages in advance so they can have extra time to process the information. Sometimes, just asking EAL students to read the topic sentence first can help them get the gist of a passage before they start note-taking.

Early-acquisition EAL learners will need some additional help, and will find it difficult to sort out the main content words (nouns, verbs, adjectives). To support them in listening and note-taking, try activating prior knowledge with diagrams and pictures, establishing a clear purpose for note-taking, modelling the process, and providing a scaffold for focused listening such as a note-taking frame.

You might also ask students to listen to a talk or watch a video with a list of keywords to tick off as they hear them, or use coloured highlighters for different parts of speech to help extract key information. Provide a graphic organiser (Idea 34) that matches the organisation of the text so it is easy to record the notes, and use symbols, visuals and sentence starters to help.

Supporting writing

Part 6

Teaching sequence for writing

'So many of our EAL learners are fluent speakers in most everyday school situations but their writing is so far behind.'

Many subject teachers find it hard to know the best way to support orally fluent EAL learners who are under-attaining in formal exam conditions.

The teaching sequence for writing draws on genre theory (Rose and Martin, 2012) and is a staged, explicit process suitable for introducing a new text type or type of writing to more advanced EAL learners. The critical stages are: exploring features and drawing attention to the form and structure of the expected written piece; and demonstrating how to write in front of the students. EAL learners will also need a lot more support at the start of the process to clarify the cultural or content knowledge needed for the task.

1 **Establish clear aims.** The teacher shares with the students the purpose, form and intended readership of the piece of writing which students will undertake, e.g. a newspaper article.
2 **Provide examples.** The students read examples of similar kinds of text.
3 **Explore the features of the text.** In the context of shared reading, the typical features of this kind of text are identified, e.g. the use of past tense, the use of emotive language.
4 **Define the conventions.** The teacher lists on the board the key features of this type of writing and ensures that students understand them.

5 **Demonstrate how it is written.** The teacher demonstrates how to write this kind of text through shared writing in front of the class. Typically, the teacher begins writing the first few sentences of the text on the board, thinking aloud to show students how and why they are making certain choices of words and sentence patterns.

6 **Compose together.** Students join in with the process of composition by suggesting words, phrases or sentences that the teacher then adds to the text.

7 **Scaffold first attempts.** Students begin their writing but some are given additional support such as a writing frame or from the teacher or from peers through guided group work.

8 **Independent writing.** Students complete the writing task independently.

9 **Draw out key learning.** This is a review process designed to secure in the students' minds what they have learnt from the writing.

Teaching tip

Allow students to use L1 during their first attempts.

Using subject-specific models (text types)

'When my teacher shows us an example of the writing, I find it much easier to know how to start.'

Most EAL learners who have had a previous education will be familiar with using models to support them with writing in their own language. They can continue this practice in English.

Teacher modelling is an essential stage in the teaching of writing, whatever the subject. For example, a written conclusion at the end of a history essay is quite different from a conclusion based on the findings of a science experiment.

EAL learners who appear to be orally fluent after two or three years may still be unfamiliar with the text types (genres) of the UK secondary curriculum. Therefore, the use of a clear, annotated model when introducing a new genre will help students understand what is expected. See the Online Resources for this book for an example annotated model.

Writing text type mats

'A lot of students find it hard to start writing on a large, blank page. Providing a writing mat for a specific topic or task is very supportive.'

Writing mats can include sentence starters, key vocabulary, discourse markers and even layout features.

Many EAL learners will benefit from having access to a text type mat when they are writing in a new and unfamiliar format. The most useful writing mats are A3 laminated pages containing specific language features, a writing frame or sentence starters and associated discourse markers.

It's important that this kind of resource looks 'professional' and not too cluttered. Cluster similar types of language in boxes. It can help to leave a relatively sparse area in the centre of the mat, where a learner can place a book or piece of paper without hiding the main content.

The specific content on each chart will obviously vary according to subject area and the specific text type. Content might also include success criteria, key drafting and proof-reading tips, timelines, diagrams and models. Language elements might be organised in any of the following ways:

- paragraph or whole text organisation
- sentence starters
- discourse markers
- comparative phrases to explain patterns or trends in graphs.

There are plenty of free text type models available on the internet, but you will probably want to download and adapt them to meet the specific demands of your subject and needs of your learners. See the Online Resources for this book for an example text type mat for a geography brochure.

Bonus idea ★

Produce a whole-school genre map identifying all the text types required in each year group and subject.

Using writing frames and sentence starters

'I never know how to start; it's the most hard part of writing.'

There is a place for writing frames to be used with both developing and competent EAL learners.

Writing frames are a good scaffolding strategy to be employed at the *end* of the teaching sequence (Idea 58). Develop simple frames for beginner learners who find it hard to start or sustain writing beyond a couple of sentences. Distil the scope of the frame to a few key sentences, and provide starter words and phrases to help scaffold the writing. An appropriate frame for a chronological report in history might look something like this.

To start with. . .
Then. . .
Next. . .
After that. . .
Finally. . .

More advanced learners tend to write quite well, but may have trouble organising their work or be reluctant to use less common adverbial phrases or discourse markers. Prepare a template that is organised clearly into different sections to highlight how the paragraphs might be structured. Perhaps learners have been researching a topic and need to write a persuasive letter. You have already deconstructed and modelled an example letter. A frame can be used to support the layout of the independent writing in this way:

Your view: *I think that/My view is. . .*
Your reasons: *The main reason is. . . Also. . . Moreover/additionally. . . Finally. . .*
Concluding the letter: *To sum up/To conclude, I would like. . . An acceptable solution/ compromise would/might/could be. . .*

Develop graphic texts

'My EAL beginners enjoy filling in boxes and bubbles with snippets of text and short phrases. It helps them overcome the fear of a blank piece of paper.'

Graphic texts require a limited amount of writing and are perfect for bridging the gap to more extensive pieces. It will help EAL learners if graphic texts are linked to work within the mainstream curriculum.

Encouraging EAL learners to produce their own graphic texts can support writing across the curriculum. The graphical layout acts as a storyboard around which both formal description, narrative and informal speech bubble dialogue can be constructed.

For printed versions, photocopy the relevant sections and obscure the text within the narrative boxes and speech or thought bubbles. Alternatively, for digital versions, take screenshots and edit out the relevant sections of text. The images can then be imported into a word processor, desktop publishing program or presentation package, ready for learners to type in their own texts.

There are good software packages that allow you to create graphic texts from scratch. Some, like *Kar2ouche* (http://creativeedutech. com/products/kar2ouche), contain banks of curriculum-related materials – settings, characters, props, text boxes – that can be stitched together, while other software, such as *Comic Life* (http://plasq.com), is perfect for building graphic texts using real photographs. Learners can choose from a range of graphic templates, add legends, speech or thought bubbles and develop narrative-based texts.

Teaching tip

Graphic texts can easily be enhanced by adding an oral component. An oral component could use L1, English or a combination of the two. Add sound to printed versions using MantraLingua's *PENpal*™ and talking stickers. For digital versions, take screenshots and import them into word processors like *Book Creator* to produce talking comics.

Bonus idea ★

Using digital cameras, encourage groups to take freeze-frame photographs of themselves in appropriate settings and import them into the software alongside other digital images.

Embedding grammar in context

'Khadija and Fatima both find it really hard to express uncertainty in their extended writing. It always sounds like they are sure about the conclusions of their investigation.'

Confident management of modality through choice of verbs and adverbs is a sign of mature writing. Many developing EAL learners need specific teaching in this area.

Teaching tip

Where teachers use textbooks, they could extract a short paragraph and use it to highlight specific language features such as past tense passive verbs in history, e.g. 'The archbishop was killed in the cathedral', or modal verbs to speculate about reasons, e.g. 'He could have escaped because the door was ajar'.

Research into the writing of EAL learners (e.g. Cameron, 2003) shows that less successful writers struggle with specific grammatical elements, such as:

- the correct use of adverbials
- expressing uncertainty with modal verbs
- choosing correct prepositions
- subject–verb agreement
- verb tenses and endings.

Each school will need to consider the best approach to tackling these problems for developing EAL writers, particularly those at proficiency code C (see Idea 12). Bear in mind that learners acquire language most successfully in the context of the curriculum rather than through decontextualised drills or vocabulary exercises, and that it is best practice for subject teachers to highlight the language forms used in their areas.

Language Garden (http://languagegarden.com) has been successfully used with younger EAL learners to help them develop a greater variety of sentence structures during creative writing. Using the metaphor of a growing plant, colourful branching stories can be built up in stages, modelling the differing purposes for verbs, adjectives, prepositions and so on.

Teachers can develop their own sentence patterns based on this format. A range of activities, including gap fills, dictionary tasks and the identification of parts of speech, is offered.

Substitution tables are another technique that help non-specialist teachers highlight grammatical forms used in their subject. These allow EAL learners to choose from a selection of words or phrases that follow a similar grammatical pattern.

Here is a sample substitution table to practise modal verbs:

My results show that the	powder metal material	must be could be might be	copper zinc iron

Taking it further

Read about nominalisation and its function in developing mature writers. Modelling how to turn verbs into adjectives enables less competent writers to condense long, descriptive phrases into abstract concepts, and is an essential skill for advanced EAL learners.

Dictogloss

'Dictogloss must be one of my favourite strategies for engaging EAL learners in mainstream lessons.'

This is an easily prepared activity that includes the whole class in speaking, listening and writing. It is suitable for any age group and subject.

Dictogloss is an activity that links active listening, speaking, note-taking and writing alongside curriculum delivery. It supports the acquisition of language, including vocabulary, typical phrases and discourse markers, and types of writing that are distinctive to particular subjects. In a dictogloss activity, a text is read several times to learners working first alone, then in pairs. As the activity progresses, the groups work collaboratively to piece together a similar but not identical version of the original text. While this may sound like dictation, be assured that it is not the same!

1 Read the text aloud at normal speed and encourage everyone to listen without taking notes. Then ask them to briefly discuss what they have heard in pairs.

2 Read the text a second time, slightly more slowly; allow learners to take notes, with an emphasis on more obvious elements, like facts and specific vocabulary. After this, give the pairs some more time to discuss and compare their notes.

3 Read the text a third time; students continue note-taking, but this time devote more attention to specific vocabulary and conjunctions that link ideas together.

4 Finally, put each pair with another one and allow ten to 15 minutes for the groups to produce their own version of the text as close to the original as possible.

Blogs and tweets

'My advanced EAL learners like Twitter because everyone is restricted to a limited number of characters; they say it makes them feel the same as everyone else.'

Getting learners involved in blogging is an excellent way of linking reading and writing, as well as developing learners' media-literacy skills. It also encourages students to think carefully about their audience.

Social networking tools are familiar to most learners who were born in the United Kingdom, and you may also discover that this is the case for many new-arrival learners. Some will not have had this experience or even have their own smart phone or computer, so will need a little time to adjust. Texting and messaging are easy ways to start new English learners off with recording ideas in 'print'.

Twitter's ease of use and restriction on message length is popular among educators working with learners acquiring English. By its very nature, Twitter requires learners to think about the formality of their communication, as well as about how to write concisely.

Why not set up a unique Twitter account for use with a tutor group or subject class? Using this account, you will be able to initiate different kinds of collaborative reading and writing tasks, including:

- researching definitions of new words through a 'word of the week' activity.
- summarising learning from the previous lesson.
- improving a sentence by changing or adding just one word at a time.
- building a collaborative story by taking turns at contributing to it.
- organising a poll or vote about a specific subject.

Teaching tip

Try to devise activities that require learners to write about issues from their own point of view or, alternatively, in a more factual, impartial way. Encourage learners to read each other's blogs, and add their own comments, as this can be highly motivating for them. Most VLEs support blogs, as well as *Edmodo* and a plethora of other secure educational sites.

Bonus idea ★

Older, competent EAL students will be able to set up their own blogs. Students could pick one subject to showcase; perhaps they can share their own ideas for revision, reflect on their reading, or create their own vocabulary lists and home language glossaries.

Digital writing tools

'In my language, we write from the right; these new letters are hard for me.'

Digital writing tools can be appropriate support for some EAL learners. However, certain tools used by emergent writers can be more confusing than helpful, while more advanced learners may come to rely on tools that they don't actually need. Correct use of each tool needs to be specifically taught.

Modern technology can greatly speed up the process of getting text into an editable format. Not only can you use cameras to photograph print and convert it into digital text, but the listening mode on mobile devices allows a user to speak in real time and capture their speech accurately within the software/app of choice. Slow writers and those unfamiliar with keyboards/touch-screen keyboards (soft keyboards) will really appreciate this shortcut.

For those at an earlier stage of learning English

- Learners who are newer to English often worry about the number of errors they make, as indicated by the spelling- and grammar-checking feature, so it may be best to turn off real-time error checking. Moreover, the conventions of colour underlining may be meaningless to the EAL user unless they are clearly explained.
- The 'auto-correct' feature may be helpful because it seamlessly corrects many basic errors. Freedom from the worry of making simple errors can help less confident writers focus on the more immediate task of constructing cohesive texts.
- Soft-keyboard word prediction will only be useful for those children who are beginning to read independently.

- The thesaurus will probably be unhelpful to early beginners, as it may refer learners to too many unfamiliar words.
- Text-to-speech technology can help with self-correction because it enables learners to hear what they have written and more easily spot their mistakes.

For more advanced learners

- These learners will appreciate having access to real-time spelling and grammar checking, as this will help them identify their mistakes and give them the option to make corrections.
- The thesaurus will be more useful to advanced learners, as they have a wider vocabulary and thus will be able to make more informed choices about which words to vary in their writing.
- Soft keyboards will help with in-word prediction as well as between words for thinking about the next word (based upon collocation principles).
- Be aware that overreliance on writing support tools can mask systematic errors or hide more serious problems.

Taking it further

OneNote, from *Microsoft Office*, has the capability to convert print into digital text via optical character recognition (OCR). Handwriting drawn onto a touch screen can also be converted into digital text.

Identity texts

'Children love creating their own stories, particularly when they can relate them to their individual cultural background and use their L1s.'

Identity texts are an effective way of activating prior knowledge as well as providing insights into the linguistic and cultural lives of children that often exist beyond the school gates.

Jim Cummins describes identity texts as artefacts created and owned by children that are literary mirrors, reflecting back a student's identity to the viewer/reader. Identity texts can be anything from pure text to talking books, podcasts or even digital stories. EAL learners, particularly those who are relatively new to the school, often feel that their teachers do not know enough about their lives, and this can be compounded for those at the initial stages of acquiring English.

Find opportunities for students to create identity texts; be aware that some children, particularly those with complex backgrounds, may be uncomfortable with the idea, and you might need to talk about and read others' examples before they feel ready to write about themselves. Always encourage the use of L1 alongside English. Here are a few ideas for personal topics:

- my life before coming to the UK
- comparing my old school and new school
- the journey from my home country
- a traditional story from my culture
- what my religion means to me
- what it feels like to be bilingual
- being British and from another cultural heritage.

Find out more about Jim Cummins' ideas on identity texts here: www.curriculum.org/secretariat/files/ELLidentityTexts.pdf

Bonus idea ★

Signing up to *Storybird* also gives access to their app called *Lark*. This online tool gives access to countless images alongside contextual words. Selected words can be dragged onto the chosen image and arranged in any sequence and pattern to create a personalised narrative before sharing and/or printing.

Vocabulary

Part 7

Vocabulary development introduction

'There are so many words in English to say the same thing.'

New-to-English learners who have had a good previous education may be overwhelmed by the number of new words they need to learn. Keeping subject-specific glossaries may help.

Research into vocabulary learning suggests there is a strong reciprocal relationship between word knowledge and reading comprehension, and students with limited vocabularies read less and thus learn fewer new words. Learning vocabulary is a cumulative task – around ten exposures to a new word are needed before it is securely embedded. Teaching definitions by themselves is unlikely to enhance comprehension.

Most newly-arrived EAL learners will be highly motivated to learn new words, but after a year or two, when they have established basic, everyday communication, their vocabulary acquisition may stall. Most native speakers can get by with about 3,000 word families. This covers 80% of the words in general use (Tier 1). EAL learners in secondary school need a far larger vocabulary than this to succeed academically, with knowledge of about 10,000 word families needed to cope with the reading demands of higher education.

3 tier vocabulary model (Beck, McKeown and Kucan, 2002)

Tier 3 – Low frequency words, often subject specialist or technical vocabulary.

Tier 2 – Medium frequency words, such as general academic language.

Tier 1 – High frequency words; everyday vocabulary.

Using word lists and glossaries

'In my science lessons, I used to write down every new word in my vocabulary book and then at the weekend I'd look them up in the Turkish dictionary and learn them all.'

Older, advanced EAL learners need to be supported to make a conscious effort to learn and consolidate new words across all curriculum areas.

The New General Service List (NGSL) (www. newgeneralservicelist.org) contains nearly 3,000 of the most frequent word families in English spoken and written texts; the New Academic Word List (NAWL) (www. newgeneralservicelist.org/nawl-new-academic-word-list) contains 960 word families from English academic papers and textbooks. Together, these two word lists cover 92% of words in academic texts in English. A word family contains all the related parts of speech for one word root (e.g. *classify, classified, classification, classifiable*).

EAL students in secondary schools need to move beyond the NGSL to learn both the specific words related to their subjects and the academic word list as this consists of the cognitive academic language for learning and higher education. Try giving your more advanced EAL learners a vocabulary test as this may well reveal a shortfall in their academic vocabulary.

Many students with previous education can work on extending vocabulary alone, with access to a bilingual dictionary and a work book in which to record the lists, but it's good practice for all teachers to build some vocabulary teaching games and strategies into their lessons (see Idea 72).

Taking it further

Visit the University of Nottingham's Academic Vocabulary website (www.nottingham.ac.uk/alzsh3/acvocab) for ideas for increasing vocabulary size.

Bonus idea ★

Try giving students a cloze exercise (Idea 54) to complete to check reading understanding. Take out 1 in 20 words (5%) randomly and see if the reader can get the gist and fill in the missing words. It is best to remove the content words (nouns, verbs, adjectives) so the context is clear enough to make meaning. Learners can also work in pairs orally to find out which words fit in the gaps. Don't always restrict them by giving a list of words to insert. Allow them to discuss all possibilities.

Alphabetical order (it's different in other languages!)

'The new student from Bangladesh is so slow using a bilingual dictionary that I don't usually bother to give her one.'

EAL learners who are literate in their L1 may be unfamiliar with English alphabetical order if their own language is written in a different script. They need support and practice with using an English dictionary.

Taking it further

Kenneth Katzner's book, *Languages of the World*, has text excerpts in many languages; you can use it for initial assessment of prior learning as well as finding out more about students' other languages. Also check out the Omniglot website (www.omniglot.com), which is full of useful facts and information about a multitude of languages and scripts.

Our alphabet has 26 letters. Most European languages use similar letters, with some additions and modifications, so it is not too difficult for European EAL learners to transfer their mother tongue dictionary skills into English. However, several European languages and most Middle Eastern or Asian languages are written in a different script, e.g. Arabic, Russian or Gujarati.

Arabic and Urdu are both Indo-European languages, but have a different type of alphabet called an abjad. Both languages are written right to left, so the dictionary order, while related to the Roman alphabet that we use, starts at the other end of the book. This can be confusing to learners who are new to reading English.

Other languages are either syllabic or logographic (e.g. Mandarin Chinese) and the letter order in a dictionary is quite different. See the example from Bengali below. The 'alphabet' is actually a syllabary of consonants with attached vowels. Hindi and Gujarati follow a similar pattern.

ক	ka	প	pa
চ	ca	য	ya
ট	ṭa	শ	śa
ত	ta	য়	ya

Vocabulary teaching

'I often ask parents to talk through some keywords before an upcoming lesson – it is generally best if they do this in their own first languages.'

Pre-teaching vocabulary to EAL learners before the main content of a lesson helps them overcome the dual challenge of learning new subject content alongside new linguistic structures.

All teachers can focus on defining and clarifying task instruction words used in their subject. Each subject could display a list of common instruction words and ask students to write their personal definitions. In maths, for example, common question words include 'indicate', 'demonstrate', 'solve', 'estimate' and 'calculate'. But what about 'insert', 'sketch', 'construct' and 'plot'? These words might be less familiar to EAL learners and they also have different meanings in other contexts, which may make them hard to interpret.

However vocabulary teaching is organised, it's important that learners encounter new language within a curriculum-related context so that meaning is explicit. In addition, the keywords will be best acquired when learners can repeatedly hear, read and use unfamiliar words in both writing and new situations.

Using wider reading to grow vocabulary 'naturally' works well if the text chosen is at just the right level with not more than 5% of the words unknown. Paying attention to context using background knowledge or visuals, such as science diagrams, helps to clarify meaning. This strategy works well for an EAL learner who has studied the topic before and can work out meanings using existing knowledge.

Taking it further

EAL learners who speak European languages, and even some South Asian languages, will find cognate vocabulary (similar root words) in many subjects. Research cognates online and discuss them with your whole class.

Bonus idea ★

You can also try direct instruction in subject areas. Try pre-teaching words, orally or using a bilingual dictionary or glossary. Morphology and word-building knowledge can be demonstrated using prefixes, suffixes and root words.

Vocabulary strategies and games

'Emre's scientific knowledge is way ahead of his peers. But his lack of vocabulary really frustrates him because he can't fully express what he knows.'

Learning lots of words is a pointless activity unless it supports wider academic learning. Vocabulary should be taught in the context of the curriculum.

Teaching tip

Use technology to assist in easy development of vocabulary games. *Osric's Bingo Card Generator* is a web-based tool that enables easy production of uniquely different bingo cards. There are two versions – one uses words only and the other allows the use of images (www.osric.com/bingo-card-generator and www.osric.com/bingo-card-generator/images.html).

Pre-teaching new language should be fun and interactive. These strategies can be introduced as lesson starters or to summarise and consolidate new learning at the end of any lesson.

- Prepare a set of 'connection cards' ready for a language-based starter activity. Connection cards are matching pairs, e.g. vocabulary and definitions or top-and-tail sentences. Give learners a connection card each, and encourage them to find the matching card. At the end of a set time, get each learner pair to read out their matched cards to check that they are correct.
- A bingo starter activity is an excellent way to recap a previous lesson. Create a set of bingo cards based upon key vocabulary, and a set of definitions to read out during the bingo activity. Play the game until someone 'wins'. Go through each definition to ensure the keywords are matched correctly.
- 'Topic taboo' is based on a commercially available card game. Each card features a topic word/phrase and a number of 'forbidden' words/phrases written below. Playing in teams, a student must describe their word/phrase to their team without using any of the 'forbidden' words. To play on an equal footing with non-EAL peers, EAL learners may be allowed to use one or more

of the forbidden words (at the discretion of the teacher). Older students can make their own cards for a specific topic and then play their game in pairs or teams.

- To recap learning at the end of a lesson, try the 'Generation game' activity. Prepare a *PowerPoint* visual containing all the language elements and other information relevant to a topic. This can be set up in various ways. Convey each idea on its own slide using appropriate text, images and sounds. Set the presentation to play automatically, so that each slide remains on screen for a set amount of time before giving way to the next. Alternatively, set a number of images to cross a slide one by one using the animation feature. When the presentation is over, ask learners to try to remember as many pieces of language or information as possible.

Bonus idea ★

EAL learners may be very good at rote learning if they have come from education systems that value this method. Draw on this learning skill to give them lists of words to learn every week.

Word building and morphology (Latin and Greek)

'Now I know why bilingual means speaking two languages – "bi" means "two" and "lingua" means "tongue"; both parts of the word come from Latin.'

Approximately 80% of the vocabulary of mathematics, science and technical English derives from Latin or Greek (often via French).

The Oxford Dictionary includes 10,500 words of Greek origin, which constitute 21.6% of the dictionary. Being able to interpret these words is essential for developing understanding in many subjects – most notably science and maths. Make sure EAL learners know how to separate the prefix, base word and suffix (which shows its grammatical form):

Root or base: Struct (build) – con**struct**, de**struct**ion, in**struct**, ob**struct**ion

Prefix: Sym/syn (with) – **syn**thesise, **sym**metry, **sym**biosis

Suffix: Instruct (verb) – instruct**or** (noun, person), instruc**tion** (abstract noun)

Learning the Latin and Greek number/quantity words goes a long way too. See the Online Resources for a printable list.

For example, ask students to explore all the words we use with 'kilo' or 'mille' in them (1000 in Greek and Latin respectively). Science teachers will also need to teach the specific scientific suffixes such as -ate and -ify.

Word clouds

'Word clouds are perfect for displaying key topic vocabulary because all the common words can be removed from a text, leaving behind the most important keywords.'

Word clouds can be produced by online tools; they enable a user to produce a cluster of words based on the frequency of those words in a digital text (including words in different languages).

The ability to visually produce word clouds, where the size of each word indicates how frequently it appears in a text, is particularly supportive of language learning because it can focus attention on subject-specific vocabulary and academic process words/phrases, tense, cohesive devices and the interconnectedness of related words. This technique is particularly good for more advanced learners of English.

At the beginning of a new piece of work, try producing a word cloud from a topic summary or essay that covers the salient points; learners can pick out some of the key vocabulary and check the meaning if needed. Ask them to predict the genre and text type that the text has been drawn from. Opinion-based texts can be studied using this technique in order to support learners' understanding of the particular position taken by the author, and two or more word clouds can be compared in order to demonstrate how word usage changes according to era, genre or text type. Personal writing can be analysed to support redrafting, e.g. by showing how lower-level writing might have an overabundance of certain verbs, adjectives or common conjunctions, such as 'and' (settings may need changing to allow 'common words' to be displayed).

Teaching tip

Let students make their own word clouds to consolidate learning of topic vocabulary. Encourage them to edit their word lists and play around with the font style and colour scheme as this will teach them about media literacy.

Taking it further

Topic word clouds can also be used as quick revision guides.

Bonus idea ★

Suggested online word cloud tools include *Wordle* (www.wordle.net) and *Wordsift* (www.wordsift.com), or try using word cloud programs such as *Wordart.com* as these allow a user to wrap the text inside an appropriate shape to add visual pizazz to their word clouds.

Collocation – what is it?

'I can never remember: "big mistake" or "large mistake". . . ?'

Collocation describes the tendency for certain words and phrases to occur next to each other in speech and writing.

As EAL learners become more proficient in their use of language across the curriculum, they learn to build 'chunks' of language from vocabulary in their immediate lexicon. However, learning which words go naturally together and which do not can be very challenging. For example, it's more natural in English to say 'increase speed' rather than 'raise speed', although the use of the word 'raise' in this context is quite logical. Ensure any work on collocations has a clear context, and develop curriculum-related activities, including highlighting incorrect collocations or matching collocations with meanings. Point out groups of colloquial collocations that are idiomatic in nature, e.g. 'give and take' and 'give notice', and get learners to build up academic collocation lists. Encourage the use of advanced internet search tools – more hits means a phrase is more widely used. Note that it's vital to enclose the two words in inverted commas and install and use concordance software, which is useful for showing collocation and analysing texts relating to different subjects. Experiment with online visual dictionaries, such as *Visual Thesaurus* (looking up 'move' returns a number of links, including 'move on', 'move up', 'move out', 'move over') or play word associations around the class (brick. . . wall. . . in. . . touch. . . type. . . written, etc.).

EAL in subject areas

Part 8

English

'I don't like studying Shakespeare because he uses so many strange words. It's not like learning English, but more like another foreign language.'

EAL learners may benefit from watching a film or reading a graphic version of the play before reading Shakespeare in the original language.

English subject lessons are particularly difficult for EAL learners, even those who are well advanced. This is partly because of the challenging literary texts on the syllabus, some written in archaic language, but also because there is no defined subject content. English language exams expect young people to comprehend extended writing on any unseen subject matter. The texts may come from an unfamiliar culture too and in recent years also including pre-19th century non-fiction. English literature also includes pre-19th century fiction and drama as well as Shakespeare, all of which can present considerable challenges to the EAL learner.

It can be argued that English (rather than the more common MFL) is the best subject to withdraw beginners from, so that they can work on the language at the appropriate level with a specialist language teacher, rather than wading through complex extended texts and attempting to write before they are ready. However, it is also possible to support the EAL learner in class with abridged or graphic texts (Idea 62).

There are many commercial support materials available for the classic English texts and, of course, Shakespeare plays have been translated into many other world languages. Use the British Council teaching resources for introducing Shakespeare to non-native speakers of English (www.teachingenglish.org.uk/teaching-teens/uk-culture). See also *No Fear Shakespeare,* which puts the modern text next to the original (http://nfs.sparknotes.com) and *Cutting Edge* publications (www.cuttingedgepublications.com/index.html).

Poetry lessons may also be very difficult for beginner EAL learners, because of the metaphorical and idiomatic language. But try starting a lesson with some poetry in the student's first language, as a way of understanding metaphor, rhyme and metre. You could ask them to try to translate it into English. Many poetic forms have been borrowed from other cultures anyway, so what better way to bring a global dimension into your curriculum?

Taking it further

There are several online resources for bilingual poetry such as www.poetrytranslation.org/poems and www.lyrikline.org/en.

Mathematics

'Why do we have to do these crazy questions about cards and dice? They make no sense to me.'

EAL learners may be unfamiliar with maths topics that are taught in the UK so it's not just the vocabulary that needs additional support.

Mathematics provides a good example of the importance of teaching language alongside curriculum content. There is evidence that many EAL learners, as well as their monolingual peers, under-attain because of the complex linguistic and literacy demands of the maths curriculum.

Mathematics is often described as a universal language. However, the topics taught in the UK may be unfamiliar to EAL students who have been educated in the Middle East, for example. While algebra and geometry are universally studied, they may have missed other topics completely, e.g. statistics and probability, so there are potential cultural barriers as well as linguistic ones.

Here are some other issues that may need attention:

- See whether learners are familiar with the Hindu-Arabic numerals, as they may have used other number systems in their country of origin. In Bengali script, the number 4 looks like our 8, which can lead to much confusion.
- Clarify how decimal points and multiplication and division signs look in the UK, as symbols differ in their use from country to country.
- Expect many maths diagrams and visuals to be unfamiliar, e.g. number lines, plans of rooms, stem-and-leaf diagrams, etc.

- Encourage EAL learners with good maths skills to use their own way of solving number problems even though their methods may be very different to those taught in UK schools.
- In some cultures, learners rely upon one secure method of solving a problem and may find it difficult to understand the notion of trying alternative methods.

Specific ideas to support curriculum access include the following:

- Provide plenty of opportunity to talk about mathematics problems and explain how they can be solved.
- Show learners how word problems work generically so they can find the essential maths content more easily.
- Focus on academic vocabulary, e.g. the many different terms for each of the number operations (take away, subtract, minus, less than, etc.).
- Highlight language anomalies – homophones such as 'sine' and 'sign', or homonyms like 'mean', 'power' and 'root', which have several different meanings.

Taking it further

Take a look at this non-verbal maths test from France, which is useful for assessing the potential of new-to-English students (http://www.cndp.fr/entrepot/fileadmin/pdf_vei/realites_pratiques/PDF_guide_scolarisation/Fiche_26_NB.pdf).

Science

'In Afghanistan, my favourite subject was maths, but I did not know much science. Now I can understand physics, but I need support for chemistry because I have never worked with chemicals before.'

EAL learners who have not studied triple science before may need additional curriculum support for certain topics.

Teaching tip

Give new EAL learners an induction lesson to cover potential hazards in a science laboratory, e.g. through identifying and describing unsafe behaviour in a picture, and writing simple DO and DON'T rules.

Taking it further

The language of science can be difficult for new EAL learners. It's not only the subject-specific vocabulary that is challenging, but also the sentence structure, e.g. the passive voice is used widely in sentences such as, 'salt *is extracted* from sea water through evaporation'. Comparative language is also difficult, so make sure you teach new EAL learners how to compare objects in terms of size, weight, appearance and so on, e.g. 'the cheetah *runs faster* than the zebra' or sentences like '*as the mass increases, the speed decreases*'.

Most science subjects provide a meaningful context for learning English. The lessons are often practical and well-illustrated with visual support, diagrams and graphical or tabular information. Additionally, most older EAL learners will have learned some science in school already and will have subject knowledge that is easily transferable. New students should be assessed carefully before placement in science groups to find out what topics they have studied before and at what level. This can be done using bilingual or L1 diagrams and not relying on pen-and-paper tests.

Biology or human and environmental sciences are taught widely in high schools across the world, but new EAL learners from less economically developed countries may not have experienced science practical work or been in a science lab before. Science safety lessons should be provided as part of the school induction process, covering the basics of behaviour in the lab and an outline of the process of scientific investigation.

Reading explanations in science is not like reading in English lessons, and EAL learners at all levels will benefit from active reading strategies such as DARTs (Idea 54) and an opportunity to transfer information from prose to a table or diagram. Beginner learners can be asked to label diagrams in their first language, thus drawing on existing knowledge, before learning the English terminology.

History

'They think I do not understand history, but my country was in the war too. Only the words are different, not the experiences of the people.'

EAL learners from Europe may have considerable prior knowledge of relevant history topics and can overcome the linguistic challenges of the subject quickly.

History has its particular issues for EAL learners. In many cases, the subject content itself is difficult for older EAL learners who have not grown up in the UK and do not have any shared cultural or historical background. But other history topics, such as the Second World War, will be familiar to most European EAL students, although it will have been taught from a completely different perspective, which may need sensitive handling.

Having EAL learners from diverse backgrounds in the history class can be immensely enriching for the teacher and students, as it will be easier to demonstrate global viewpoints of topics such as the Crusades, India, the Industrial Revolution and even migration itself.

The amount of reading and writing in history means that beginner learners may find the subject hard to access without considerable support for learning vocabulary and for reading sources that are written in archaic language. Active reading strategies are to be encouraged for all rather than a 'retreat from print', as everyone will need to work hard at understanding challenging texts.

Key visuals such as timelines, flow diagrams and, above all, images of people, places and artefacts will be essential scaffolding tools for all EAL learners.

Taking it further

Certain language features may need additional teaching, perhaps by using substitution tables (Idea 63) or grammar games. The past tense needs to be secure for writing about history – including the present and past perfect and passive forms, e.g. *she had conquered, he has surrendered, they have been defeated*. Word-building exercises are also useful for more advanced learners, who will need to be able to write about abstract processes and concepts (Idea 73). Consider teaching all new vocabulary in four forms – noun, verb, abstract noun, adjective, e.g. democrat, democratise, democracy, democratic.

Bonus idea ★

Use simplified reading text with tailored activities from sites such as the *New Internationalist Wiki* (https://eewiki.newint.org).

Geography

'I travelled across many countries to get to safety in England. I saw mountains, desert, rough sea and big roads. Now the difficult journey helps me study. '

Geography can be an enabling subject for EAL students. Many students will have lived in or travelled to other countries and can draw on those experiences.

EAL learners will bring to geography an in-depth understanding of at least one other country and its culture that can be enriching for whole-class lessons. They may have experienced different climates, natural hazards, agricultural practices, rural life, and push-and-pull factors for migration, to name but a few things. However, EAL learners who are new to the UK may know very little about the UK and Europe in terms of physical geography and places beyond their own community.

Geography is a very visual subject, making use of diagrams, maps and 3D cutaway visuals. *Google Maps™* supports the development of map skills; switching from 'map' to 'satellite view' and back again shows how maps diagrammatically relate to actual geographical features. You can also try kinaesthetic learning for key concepts, such as dense/sparse population or movements of Earth in relation to the Moon.

Through using BBC country websites, students can learn to research and note-take from a position of strength using their own country as a model. Other ideas include sorting statements (true/false/not sure) about a place (you can use a picture as a starting point); sentence starters or writing frames for comparing places; and cloze exercises for watching videos or going on trips, to encourage active listening.

Art and music

'Some of our new EAL students are talented musicians. They come to school early every day to play the piano in the foyer.'

New-to-English learners can demonstrate their talents in music and art long before they can express themselves in English. These subjects give them a chance to shine.

Art and music are subjects that may enable EAL learners to demonstrate their talents even if they cannot speak much English. However, be aware some Muslim cultures and families do not allow students to participate in music or draw representations of the human form, so newly-arrived students may not have been exposed to lessons in the creative arts before.

Teaching ideas for art/music:

- Ask learners to talk in depth about one or more images; this encourages the use of more formal talk that helps to bridge the gap between thinking, talking and writing.
- Some learners have difficulty with annotating their own artwork; reviewing each other's work helps reinforce technical language and model language structures that they will need to use in their writing.
- After a practical lesson, ask students to report back either orally or in a reflective journal about what they have done. This requires the use of the past tense (which you may need to reinforce).
- Ask fluent English speakers to create a visual (or aural) vocabulary list for new-to-English learners.
- Use listening frames when students are watching a video or listening to a piece of music.
- Use a range of different graphic organisers (Idea 34), e.g. to add statements about a composer/artist's life to a timeline.

Taking it further

Organise a cultural evening to showcase the art, music and dance of the different communities in the school. Invite all the parents, so they can get to know each other in a comfortable and enjoyable way.

Physical education

'In Lithuania, I was in the school basketball team and I was one of the top swimmers. But now it's hard for me to play cricket and rugby.'

PE and sport can be great for developing strong bonds between people from different countries and cultures, but it can be hard if successful young sports men and women cannot demonstrate their existing skills.

At first it may appear that PE is a great subject for including EAL learners with their peers, but teachers will need to ensure that adolescent EAL students are supported to join in with an existing team. In other cases, newer EAL learners will be talented in a particular sport and may need additional support and even resources so that they can participate at the highest level, such as buying specialist kit to join a cricket club.

One starting point is to find out the strengths and aptitudes of a new EAL student (sometimes literally). What sports have they tried before? Are they keener on ball games or individual pursuits? Find out what their country's national sport is and build on this; researching the national sports of different countries could be a great lesson for a rainy day.

There may be specific religious and cultural issues that are barriers to EAL students participating fully in PE. Some students will not want to change in front of their peers. It may also mean changing the dress code from shorts/short sleeves to tracksuits. Schools need to be particularly sensitive to the needs of older Muslim students during the fasting month of Ramadan when they will be fasting from dawn to dusk, which means taking nothing by mouth, including water.

Developing English in PE lessons

PE is a great subject for introducing newer EAL learners to focused listening to and giving of instructions, perhaps highlighting the cohesive devices we use for sequencing (e.g. *first*, *next*, *then*, *finally*). Being able to watch a teacher or student model an activity while talking it through is a perfect way to learn the language while doing. Another strategy is to get a more fluent student to report back to the class or group after watching a technique, thus modelling the use of the past tense, e.g. 'He **is pivoting** on his left foot; he **pivoted**'.

During PE theory lessons, the language becomes more academic, with a lot of technical vocabulary and abstract nouns for concepts, e.g. impact, volume, protection, globalisation. You may need to model these in a concrete context first. Try using some of the vocabulary teaching strategies (Idea 72) to support EAL learners with the use of more formal terms.

> **Bonus idea** ★
>
> Look out for visiting foreign teams and arrange trips to international matches so that EAL students can enjoy watching their compatriots.

Modern languages (including community languages)

'I took a GCSE in Polish after one year in England and I also studied Spanish and got a grade B after two years. Next year I'll be starting AS Polish too.'

Most older EAL learners who have literacy in their first language and basic English fluency can attain high grades in language exams.

The British Council provide some great resources for teaching Chinese language and culture (https:// schoolsonline. britishcouncil.org/ classroom-resources/ year-of-the-sheep/ teacher-resources).

Goldsmiths, University of London offers CPD certificate courses for teachers of Arabic and Chinese. The University of East London also offers a PGCE in community languages such as Russian, Bengali, Japanese and Urdu.

Make sure that new EAL learners in lower secondary school are not withdrawn from modern language lessons to learn English. They are probably more capable than most of adding languages to their existing repertoire. Older learners who are new to English may find it hard to catch up and their ability to participate fully will need to be considered on a case-by-case basis.

Schools who have high numbers of speakers of one of the community languages may decide to timetable their teaching as part of MFL to maximise their assets. Other schools offer GCSEs in other languages on an extra-curricular basis.

EAL learners are usually some of the best linguists in any school as they start with the advantage of already being fluent in another language. National attainment data suggests that EAL students are more likely to achieve the English Baccalaureate than English mother tongue students. So, it's a very good idea to make sure that all EAL students are able to access modern or community language lessons and take an exam if possible. Unfortunately, only the most common languages spoken in the UK are available from the English and Welsh exam boards. Several subjects are undergoing revision as of 2017; see the individual exam boards' websites for a list of languages currently offered.

Developing home and community partnerships

Part 9

Produce a 'how schools work' video/album

'As a parent of a newly arrived child, I had so many questions because our education system is completely different. The school produced a video answering many of these questions and I really appreciated it being in my language as well.'

New-arrival families will appreciate information about their child's new school in as accessible a format as possible. Bear in mind that this may also help established families, as moving from one school phase to the next can raise all sorts of additional questions.

Taking it further

Ask parents, bilingual practitioners and other bilingual professionals (Idea 11) to help with producing high-quality translations, and dub the video in those languages most significant to the school's context. With the help of adults, bilingual students themselves may be able to voice over the video.

Bonus idea ★

Older EAL learners may enjoy producing photo albums about their own school; ideas include identifying key staff, important rooms or areas of the building as well as information about exams, using the library, homework support, etc.

Try involving the whole school community in the production of a video to explain essential information about the British education system in general, as well as the specifics of your own school. Where possible, get learners involved in planning, filming, editing and writing or recording the narration.

The specific contents of such a video will vary from school to school, and it can sometimes be difficult to predict which elements will be helpful. Try interviewing a range of established EAL students, parents or carers to elicit what information would have been most useful in preparation for starting secondary school. There will be common elements whether the learner is British-born or newly arrived from abroad.

It may help to split the final video into different sections, so that families can access the parts that seem most relevant to them; any essential school information can go into the first section. Once it is finished, you can issue the video as a CD to all new parents or make it available via the school's website.

Engaging parents and family learning

'I never visited the school with my first child. But once I went to a numeracy workshop, I learned so much and it gave me confidence to go in again.'

While most minority ethnic parents are keen to support their child's education, others can be harder to engage. Family learning events can encourage parents to come into school and this helps community integration.

Organising family learning events is an effective way to encourage greater participation from parents or carers. You may wish to focus on parents/carers from a specific ethnic background, target families of new-arrival learners or promote community cohesion by inviting families from a variety of ethnic backgrounds including white British. Don't give up if turnout is initially low. Word gets around, and participation tends to improve the more sessions you arrange.

Family learning events can be used to:

- Provide information about the UK education system and aspects of how the school works.
- Teach parents/carers English, numeracy or computing skills.
- Give parents ideas on how to support their children with homework or exam revision.
- Help parents experience what school examinations are like.
- Explain the school's behaviour or anti-bullying policy and how to keep children safe when using the internet;
- Orient the school's position on 'British Values' within the wider context of promoting community cohesion, encouraging communication and collaboration between different cultures.

Teaching tip

How you organise family learning is another important consideration. A sequence of sessions around a particular theme is likely to have greater impact than a one-off event, and you should think about the time of day that is likely to attract the most families. Consider laying on transport or offering a crèche facility if possible.

Bonus idea ★

Conduct a survey with all parents to find out what sort of learning they would be interested in. Whatever format is used, it's important to ensure that every attempt has been made to make the survey as accessible as possible from a linguistic and cultural perspective.

Supplementary schools and achievements beyond the school

'Although I knew Hiba spoke Arabic at home, I had no idea she was studying it at Saturday school until she asked about taking Arabic GCSE the other day.'

Many children have linguistic, cultural and religious experiences that are rarely brought into school life unless robust efforts are taken to find out about them. There are clear benefits for students in terms of motivation and self-esteem when teachers credit students for these aspects of their lives.

Find out whether EAL learners are continuing to study L1 outside of school – perhaps an informal home-based approach or at weekend community language classes. In most cases, the supplementary school will welcome support from the main school including advice about exam technique and entries, and may provide additional teaching to support school curriculum subjects.

Celebrate the fact that some learners have deeply religious lives that put constraints on their home life, such as fasting during Ramadan. Such situations usually require significant discipline, and the school will need to be sensitive to these notable events. Learners may also have responsibilities at home, such as interpreting and translating for parents or caring for younger siblings and elderly relatives. Schools can support each learner's individual home circumstances through developing flexible arrangements. It is vital to keep accurate records of such information, ensuring that all relevant staff are kept informed. You should also talk to the primary school at the point of transition.

Accessing resources within the local community

'One of our parents owns a restaurant and we invited them in during international week to run a cooking masterclass for KS3.'

To ensure schools make use of the resources available through ethnic, cultural and religious groups within the local community, consider making this an SLT responsibility.

Most of the major BAME groups will have an official association that represents them. If you are seeking information about the history and culture of a specific group, then this is a good starting point. Children from service families will have local contacts from within the Ministry of Defence who can provide advice and guidance for the particular needs of these children and their families.

Audit the area for shops, businesses, and religious centres to get some useful contacts. Inviting successful role models from BAME communities to the school can enrich the curriculum and help with identifying potential speakers. You can identify suitable places for visits to support the teaching of RE, or businesses who could support areas of the curriculum and offer work experience.

Knowing the services on offer in the local authority will really benefit newly-arrived families, such as specific local services for ethnic minority families with children and young adults with disabilities; legal services and charitable groups for young people from refugee or asylum-seeking families; or local community language classes and supplementary language schools (Idea 86).

Taking it further

Make contact with your Local Authority as they will probably have lists of organisations that cater for the distinctive needs of children and families from BAME communities. Refer parents to websites such as the *British Council* (www.britishcouncil.org/english) and *English My Way* (www.englishmyway.co.uk).

Bonus idea ★

Some local colleges will offer ESOL classes. Work with them to develop clear guidelines for which type of learners to enrol in English-language courses. Certain late arrivals in KS4 may benefit from part-time attendance at college or external tutors running targeted classes in school.

Learners who take extended visits

'Sarfraz enjoyed telling us all about his visit to his grandparents in Pakistan. The whole class learned a lot as he was able to talk about the impact of the earthquake in Kashmir.'

Rather than making it a problem when children take extended visits, practitioners should treat it as a learning opportunity.

Many older EAL students still have extended family in other countries. While they can keep in touch through social media these days, young people may also take extended visits to their parents' country of origin for weddings, funerals and other important family events.

For EAL learners who do make extended visits, here are some ideas for making the most of the learning opportunities:

- Develop procedures that enable students to continue their studies while on their trip such as videoconferencing (Idea 90).
- Where possible, entrust learners with digital media equipment to take pictures or record sounds.
- Encourage learners to keep a diary or blog of their journey.
- Suggest that learners collect interesting resources to support learning for particular subject topics such as earthquakes or flooding, animal conservation, sustainable technology and primary healthcare.

When learners return, they could share their experience by giving a presentation to the class, contributing to an assembly about their country or cultural background, or making a book or diary about their time away.

School-linking projects

'Last term students from our school visited our partner school in Tanzania. It's had a positive impact on their learning in many subjects as well as encouraging several sixth formers to stand for Youth Parliament in our region.'

There can be many benefits from linking with schools locally, nationally or even internationally. Having educational links with a diverse range of schools provides opportunities to support community cohesion and develop a culturally-infused curriculum.

Global school partnerships can help young people communicate, collaborate and learn about each other, and explore global issues. They can also be very powerful ways to include learners by maintaining connections with home communities overseas, enabling the use and development of other languages and providing a vehicle for exciting curriculum work.

However, this does not happen automatically – it needs careful planning with partners, and an effective strategy so that your link provides insights into alternative perspectives and combats prejudice, racism and xenophobia. Without careful thought and consideration, it can reinforce stereotypes.

Think carefully about *why* you want to link in the first place – one recommendation is to link locally first, perhaps with a school with a different catchment of learners, or with a community in a different part of the country. Links are assumed to be made with other countries, but linking across cultures within one's own country is an effective way of learning about others and the diverse nature of our own communities, challenging assumptions and helping to break down barriers. If you are in a mainly white British, rural area, why not link with a school in a nearby multi-ethnic city?

Taking it further

Some excellent resources for linking to help you consider your next steps are available from HEC Global Learning Centre (www.globallearninglondon.org). For support with international programmes, take a look at the British Council Schools Online (https://schoolsonline.britishcouncil.org) or eTwinning, the European network for school linking (www.etwinning.net).

Videoconferencing (VC)

'Natalie was the only Lingala speaker in our school and she was isolated from her peers so we set up a regular conference for her with a school in the city which had several Congolese students.'

Videoconferencing is an essential tool for communication at a distance – locally, nationally and even internationally.

Videoconferencing enables speakers of other languages to practise their oral skills, and is perfect for learning languages in general. EAL learners can also develop questioning and interview skills in English. When learners from similar and different backgrounds can socialise together or work on curriculum-related projects within any subject area, community cohesion is enhanced. Experts from BAME communities can be 'invited' into the classroom to share skills and experiences and act as positive role models. Practitioners can also use VC to liaise together and develop their expertise in managing EAL and ethnic-minority achievement.

Tips for planning a VC session:

- Book a quiet room or area for the session.
- Ensure that all the equipment is working.
- Check that the VC client works; some schools and local authorities block certain software such as *Skype*™, although *FlashMeeting* tends to work everywhere.
- Ensure that when learners are communicating together, they are always supervised by an adult.
- Note that some VC software allows users to record the session for playback at a later date; while this can be very useful, it is important to check parental permissions when children and young people are involved.

Here are a few ideas for videoconferencing:

1 **Linking isolated EAL learners.** Many schools have relatively small numbers of BAME learners, and their EAL population may be culturally and linguistically isolated; this can also be true of their families. Try to identify same-language speakers in other isolated situations to facilitate communication through a VC link. This allows EAL learners the opportunity to practise L1 and socialise with those of a similar age and background.

2 **Community cohesion projects – linking learners from mainly white schools with those from ethnically diverse settings (and vice versa).** This is a useful way of enabling white British students to meet and interact with learners with whom they would not normally have contact because of the locality of their school or home. In this way, individuals and groups can socialise together or take part in more structured activities that look at the commonality and differences between people. It can be a useful way to prepare for learner-exchange visits and can also facilitate follow-up work.

3 **Bilingual Q&A sessions for parents of new arrivals.** Organising events where a bilingual practitioner is at the end of a VC link at a pre-arranged time can be useful to enable parents to ask questions in L1 about education and other related matters. This will help not only their school-aged children but also older siblings in terms of signposting them on to further education.

4 **Bilingual support or community language teaching.** One practitioner can efficiently deliver bilingual support or teaching in a subject area to learners in different schools. This can help raise the self-esteem of EAL learners who know the same language because they can get formal qualifications. Besides supporting language learning, this also contributes to the intercultural dimension of the curriculum.

> **Taking it further**
>
> You could also try an 'Ask the experts' session, inviting members of local community groups to become experts for the day. Using VC technology, the 'experts' can enter classrooms virtually to talk about their own expertise in work, religious practice or a creative talent. Try linking this with special celebrations or national or international events.

Whole-school approaches

Part 10

Develop an EAL policy

'The inspectors were really impressed with our EAL policy as it was clearly linked to the whole-school equality policy as well as the language and literacy policy.'

An EAL manager should consult with a range of middle managers to support writing a whole-school EAL policy to ensure it encompasses their concerns about progress and attainment.

Taking it further

A school may not necessarily require an EAL policy if other relevant policies are infused by appropriate statements, e.g. equality, assessment, teaching and learning, etc. Threading comments throughout other policies suggests a more integrated approach to practice and provision for EAL learners than having a stand-alone policy.

A school with even a few EAL learners will need to have an EAL policy. It's best practice that this sits within or alongside the equality policy. An EAL policy should articulate how the school will:

- Provide a safe and secure learning environment for all EAL learners, supporting them to become independent learners.
- Ensure there is enough curriculum support to help learners to make excellent progress.
- Group EAL learners by academic potential rather than their English language proficiency.
- Ensure high expectations and achievement for all.
- Develop links with parents and communities.

The policy should also clarify how the school will provide:

- In-depth assessment of the needs of new-arrival EAL learners.
- In-class support of EAL students.
- High-quality English language teaching.
- Training that develops subject teachers' competence in meeting the linguistic and learning needs of bilingual students in the mainstream.
- Appropriate curriculum teaching strategies and resources.
- Monitoring and evaluation of teaching programmes and student progress and attainment.

The EAL policy will also likely clarify the school's language and literacy policy regarding how EAL learners can:

- Use their existing language abilities and knowledge in different contexts, and for different and new purposes around the school.
- Meet new language in contexts that are familiar and supportive.
- Access further teaching in their mother tongue, such as GCSE and A level qualifications.

The EAL policy may also need to have regard for the additional social and pastoral support that new-to-English learners, especially refugees and asylum seekers, may need beyond the curriculum.

Bonus idea ★

Make time to support faculties, pastoral and subject staff to embed aspects of the EAL policy into their own departmental policies and plans.

IDEA 92

Managing whole-school EAL provision

'All schools will benefit from a senior manager who leads on ethnic minority achievement (EMA) and, if necessary, EAL.'

Many schools, particularly those with significant numbers of EAL learners, build a team of specialist staff to develop sound EAL practice.

Taking it further

Work with a member of the SLT to build a team of EAL champions from different subject areas, in order to support you across the school to embed teaching strategies and inclusive approaches more widely.

Any school with more than a few EAL learners is likely to need to appoint a coordinator or manager to organise provision. Here are some pointers for teachers in this role:

- Clearly identify roles and responsibilities within the school so that the key tasks do not fall upon the shoulders of just one person.
- Develop a specific policy for EAL (Idea 91) and/or ensure that references to BAME/EAL are made within all relevant policies.
- Audit the school population and ensure that the student-level data captures ethnicity, date of arrival in the UK, L1, religion, country of origin and other essential information.
- Develop tracking systems to monitor both attainment and progress of BAME and EAL learners; you need to be able to make comparisons between different ethnic and linguistic groups as well as identify the rate of progress for individual learners.
- Map support provision across the whole school and allocate staff to work with specific subjects or teachers rather than only supporting new-to-English students.
- Establish a programme of continuing professional development (Idea 100) for all the staff; training should include a focus on strategies to support different stages of EAL learners and on how to promote cultural diversity through the curriculum.

Bonus idea ★

Decide whether it is appropriate to timetable additional lessons for English and GCSE option support for late-arriving EAL students and some intervention or catch-up lessons for those who have limited previous education.

Planning and timetabling withdrawal/intervention

'Some of our newer EAL learners have hardly been to school before because of the breakdown in education in their war-torn country. We made changes to our timetables to make sure they had enough support.'

Schools may need to make an additional provision for new-to-English students who have missed some primary education.

Any additional, small-group teaching for older students should be carefully planned to ensure they don't miss essential curriculum learning. There is a place for *some* small-group teaching outside the mainstream classroom, especially for those students significantly behind age-related expectations in many subjects and/or those who have entered UK education in Year 10 or later. However, all withdrawal teaching should be linked closely to the work of the mainstream class through content-led language teaching.

A school might need to consider the following when assessing the need for intervention:

- What additional catch-up lessons are needed for EAL learners who have missed some of their primary education?
- Which EAL students will benefit from having some time outside the mainstream class with a specialist English teacher?
- Do some EAL students need a quiet place to relax with supportive peers or adults after speaking in another language all day long?
- Can the school provide a dedicated room with books, computers, games and maybe even tea or soft drinks?
- Do you have refugee students or those who have had disrupted education who may need additional pastoral support?

Teaching tip

Additional reading lessons for literate EAL learners, those who can already read in their own language, are best separated from native English speakers with specific literacy difficulties. They will not need much support for decoding but may need help with pronunciation or additional time to learn vocabulary. EAL learners who cannot read in any language may need one-to-one teaching.

Bonus idea

Organise a member of staff to run a homework club a few days a week so students can get support after school too. Many new EAL students will find themselves in temporary or crowded accommodation where it is hard to study.

Option support for vulnerable students

'Last year we admitted nine new students into Year 10. They all had unique needs and we had to make changes to our timetable to make sure they had enough support.'

Schools may need to make an additional support plan and recruit new staff to meet the needs of EAL learners who are late arrivals.

Taking it further

Try linking up EAL teachers and subject teachers, e.g. some maths topics, such as time or probability, can be very difficult both conceptually and linguistically. Working together, the maths teacher and EAL teacher can plan a session covering both the additional content and language for probability. (See Idea 77.)

Bonus idea ★

Offering an 'option support slot' on the main GCSE timetable is a good way of helping the more vulnerable students settle in. Ideally, this should complement the work of the mainstream; it could be led by an EAL teacher but draw on other subject teachers (especially from maths and science) to plan and even deliver lessons.

Joining a new school in Year 10 or 11 can be very difficult for all but the most able EAL students who have a strong grasp of English. It is not just the language that is a barrier to high attainment, but different subjects, syllabuses and types of exams can be daunting, especially when courses have already started in Year 9. It is good if a school can be flexible in arrangements for accommodating older, more vulnerable students. Their exam results do not need to be included in reporting, so they do not affect overall progress data. It can be incredibly rewarding to see a withdrawn or traumatised young person settle, develop and form good relationships, even if their results do not compare with their peers.

The EAL teacher may concentrate on generic skills of reading for information, unpacking exam questions, learning subject vocabulary, writing clear paragraphs with topic sentences, or note-taking. The subject teachers can pre-teach or revise key exam topics so the EAL learner gets a second chance to process new language in context.

See the Online Resources for a model EAL curriculum plan.

Training and coaching all staff

'Every year the EAL coordinator runs a twilight training session for newly qualified teachers and other staff who are new to the school.'

The quality of training about EAL in initial teacher education is variable and new staff in the early part of their careers may need to be reminded of the distinctive approaches to teaching students with EAL.

A school with BAME students and EAL learners will need to provide additional training to all new staff in order to develop their skills and confidence in working with a diverse student body. Newly qualified and trainee teachers may not have had much time on their courses or school placements to look specifically at the needs of EAL learners, and will appreciate having a deeper understanding of the languages and communities of their new school. Other new staff may have moved from a part of the UK with less ethnic diversity and need time to adapt their planning and pedagogy to a different student cohort. Some schools may be experiencing rapid demographic change due to migration patterns, and even the most experienced staff may need to refresh and rethink some approaches.

The following topics and themes are good starting points for whole-school training:

- A summary of the languages and countries of origin of the school cohort.
- An introduction to the key principles of second language acquisition, e.g. BICS, CALP and the importance of using L1 (Idea 23).
- A summary of the EAL proficiency stages and their implication for classroom practice.
- Tips about planning subject lessons with language objectives.
- Resources and materials to support reading for information and extended writing.
- Practice in trying out vocabulary teaching strategies (Ideas 71 and 72).

Taking it further

Teacher coaching is a supportive individual approach to CPD. It involves an experienced practitioner working with a colleague on planning, co-teaching, modelling new strategies and reflective evaluation across a series of lessons. The focus could be integrating EAL beginners, or perhaps developing formal writing. This approach is valuable because it is hands-on and practical; provides sustainability; embeds effective teaching strategies; disseminates good practice across departments; provides a safe space for teachers to innovate and experiment; gives teachers supportive feedback; has significant impact for individual teachers and potentially the whole school.

Using the curriculum to reflect the cultures of the school

'I was really excited when my science teacher talked about the discoveries of the Persian scientist, Ibn Sina, in our lesson because we studied him in my own country.'

All staff can enable EAL learners to draw on their prior knowledge and educational experiences to embed a global dimension in subject lessons.

Taking it further

For free, downloadable teaching materials that are sortable by age, key stage, subject and theme, see https://globaldimension.org.uk.

Students need to see their linguistic and cultural heritage reflected in the curriculum in order for them to feel valued and welcome. It's important for all schools, no matter the diversity of their intake, to provide a culturally rich curriculum that reflects the diverse nature of the UK and enables all students to learn about the world's interconnections.

The National Curriculum provides the core of what schools are expected to provide for their students, and offers a starting point for studying and understanding the diverse nature of the UK. Schools can include opportunities within the curriculum and through wider learning opportunities, e.g. celebrate Black History Month or study the contribution that Islamic scholarship has made to science. This is perhaps even more important for those schools who have few or no students from these heritages.

The curriculum can be enhanced to reflect the cultures of the students in school. While some subjects may lend themselves more easily to this than others, it is more than possible to enhance the curriculum in diverse ways through teachers' reflective planning and resourcing, so that it is both motivating and relevant to young BAME and EAL students' needs and interests.

The role of modern languages in maintaining and sustaining community languages has been covered elsewhere in this book (Idea 83), but here are some more ideas for how to use the curriculum to reflect and celebrate the cultures of the EAL students in your school. Topics could include:

- civil rights struggle in the US and South Africa in history, linking with modern civil rights movements today
- the global fashion industry, ethics and trade in geography
- commonalities in faith studies, e.g. pilgrimage
- world music and the origins of modern-day music genres
- food, cooking and cultural traditions from students' own families in food technology
- critical thinking in a study of the media
- real-world maths problems
- teaching the Holocaust and linking to prejudice, intolerance and community cohesion.

All of these will enable the whole school community to understand the importance of respecting similarities and differences, as well as appreciating diverse and multiple perspectives on global issues and how identities affect opinions.

Bonus idea ★

More fluent EAL students will be able to contribute their own cultural knowledge and skills into the curriculum, e.g. demonstrating a dance; researching and presenting about historical figures; translating poems from other languages.

Conducting a learning environment walk

'It was very revealing to walk around the school with a parent and see everything through their eyes.'

Experience suggests that a learning environment audit is best performed by two or more people – perhaps a senior leader and a governor with responsibility for inclusion. It's also worth involving BAME parents and the school council.

How welcoming does the school feel to people from BAME backgrounds? This is important, because the learning environment communicates something about the school's attitude towards inclusion in its widest sense.

The school office is often the first point of contact for many families and a good place to start the 'walk'. What is your immediate impression as you enter this area? Are there dual-language welcome signs? Does the library stock a good range of dual-language dictionaries, bilingual books and stories from other cultures? Are materials routinely checked to avoid stereotype and/or tokenism? What about the corridors, classrooms and other school areas? Look out for these elements:

- intercultural displays that demonstrate the school's commitment to developing a culturally-infused curriculum
- dual-language material that celebrates the many languages used within the school community
- photographs of people drawn from a range of ethnic backgrounds
- classroom organisation that shows evidence of flexibility in grouping arrangements for all learners.

Running the Young Interpreter Scheme®

'I got picked to be a Young Interpreter because I have lots of different qualities: I speak several languages but I am also a good listener and enjoy helping people.'

The Young Interpreter Scheme® capitalises on the immense potential within each school to use the linguistic and social skills of all their learners to develop an inclusive and welcoming environment for EAL learners and their families.

Training forms an essential part of the scheme. The scheme is most effective when bilingual learners are trained alongside non-EAL students. Confident bilingual students learn how to utilise their L1 skills to assist with interpreting when working with beginner EAL learners, particularly new arrivals and their families. English-only speakers work alongside bilingual peers to employ strategies and resources for giving support in situations where an L1 is not shared between students and adults.

Such a scheme goes way beyond arranging peer buddies (Idea 6) for new-arrival EAL learners. Potential activities permeate the whole school, from promoting cultural and linguistic diversity to working with families and supporting individual EAL learners in and out of the classroom.

Potential activities can include the following:

- showing visitors and new-arrival families around the school
- inducting and settling new learners
- using interpreting skills to facilitate home–school communication
- supporting peers in the classroom
- offering taster language sessions for peers and school staff.

Teaching tip

Young Interpreters should not be used as a replacement for professional adult interpreters, or get significantly involved in translation work. Further guidance about this issue can be accessed here: http://www3.hants.gov.uk/education/emtas/supportinglanguages/pupilinterpreters.htm.

Taking it further

Hampshire Ethnic Minority and Traveller Achievement Service (EMTAS) has developed a fully-fledged Young Interpreter Scheme®. All the training materials can be accessed online here: http://www3.hants.gov.uk/education/emtas-2/goodpractice-2/hyis.htm. Alternatively, you can follow them on Twitter @YIscheme and on Facebook (www.facebook.com/Young-Interpreter-Scheme-1393344670884345).

Six of the best from the internet

'The internet is a treasure trove of useful sites for this area of work.'

Don't underestimate the value of learning from others. There are websites, news groups and resource repositories that can provide invaluable support for busy teachers.

1 National Association for Language Development in the Curriculum (NALDIC)
www.naldic.org.uk

This is one of the most comprehensive websites around, offering a good balance between theoretical research and practical teaching and learning pedagogy. While there is some open access material, most of the downloadable articles, documents and media clips only become available upon payment of an annual membership fee.

2 The EAL MESHGuide
www.meshguides.org/guides/node/112

As stated on the website, *'This guide is written principally to support teachers and learning support assistants working with EAL learners in any educational setting and who are at any stage of fluency in the learning of English.'*

3 EAL Nexus
https://ealresources.bell-foundation.org.uk/

A partnership between the British Council and The Bell Foundation, this website is a single point of contact for EAL resourcing and pedagogy. As well as information pages and downloadable teaching resources, there are also some interesting research reports and video case studies.

4 The Collaborative Learning Project
www.collaborativelearning.org

This site hosts activities created by teachers for teachers. Developed over many years, it is a cornucopia of downloadable activities aimed at developing the oral skills of EAL learners.

5 EMTAS4Success (a local authority website)
www.sgsts.org.uk/SupportForVulnerablePupils/EMTAS/SitePages/Home.aspx

It's worth doing a search for relevant local-authority websites around the United Kingdom – there may well be one for your area. An internet search for keywords like 'ethnic minority achievement service' will find most of them. There are many notable sites, but 'EMTAS4Success' is a particularly rich resource with many downloadable guidance documents.

6 Hampshire Ethnic Minority Achievement Service (EMTAS) – online EAL eLearning
http://emtas.hias.hants.gov.uk/course/view.php?id=19

The Hampshire EMTAS EAL eLearning involves interactive online training units that cater for the needs of EAL learners, aimed at teachers, TAs, inclusion managers and governors, with particular relevance for NQTs and trainee teachers.

Each unit is self-certificated upon completion. Topics covered include: bilingualism, working with parents, the SEND–EAL interface, culturally inclusive schools, and teaching and learning, among many others.

> **Bonus idea**
>
> Build up your own list of the most useful websites and distribute them amongst staff, either in document format or a set of weblinks.

Professional networking and CPD

'Regularly meeting EAL professionals at network meetings has given me so much confidence as the EAL coordinator at my school.'

All staff need access to high-quality CPD as pedagogy and resources inevitably change and develop over time. Training could be face-to-face, network meetings or longer-term accredited training.

Finding local EAL advice and guidance can be difficult, and you may need to research what resources are available either regionally or via online networks. Here are a few ideas to get you started:

- Join NALDIC – National Association for Language Development In the Curriculum. Membership benefits include full access to their website, free copies of the *EAL Journal* (a termly magazine of practice, research and activism) and discounts for the annual conference.
- Look out for networks of professionals that meet from time to time in and around your area. TeachMeets sometimes have a focus on EAL, and NALDIC supports Regional Interest Groups (RIGs) all over the country.
- Check out what's available online, as universities, non-government organisations, teacher unions and charities sometimes offer free EAL CPD.
- It is also worth connecting with relevant organisations on Facebook and following EAL professionals on Twitter.
- NASSEA is the professional hub for the EMA practitioners in North of England: http://nassea.org.uk.
- SATEAL is the EAL professional body for Scotland: www.sateal.org.uk.
- EALAW is the EAL professional body for Wales: www.ealaw.org.uk/index.php/about-ealaw.

Taking it further

Join EAL-Bilingual, an online professional email network for all things connected with EAL and bilingual teaching and learning. You can join here: https://groups.google.com/forum/#!forum/eal-bilingual

Bonus idea ★

Many universities run masters-level accredited face-to face or distance learning courses connected with bilingual education/EAL matters. While this can be professionally developing for any school-based practitioner, it may be essential for an EMA coordinator or to become an EAL adviser within a local authority. For information, visit: https://naldic.org.uk/professional-learning-cpd.

References and further reading

Barwell, R. (2001). 'Word problems', *What Works? Research into Practice*, 34. Available at: http://www.edu.gov.on.ca/eng/literacynumeracy/inspire/research/WW_Word_Problems.pdf.

Beck, I. L., McKeown, M. G. & Kucan, L. (2002). 'Choosing words to teach', in *Bringing Words to Life: Robust Vocabulary Instruction*. New York, NY: Guilford Press.

Bialystok, E. (2009). 'The good, the bad, and the indifferent', *Bilingualism: Language and Cognition* 12(1), pp. 3–11.

Cameron, L. (2002). 'Measuring vocabulary size in English as an additional language', *Language Teaching Research*, 6(2) pp. 145–173.

Cameron, L. (2003). *Writing in English as an Additional Language at Key Stage 4 and Post-16*. London: Ofsted. Available at: www.naldic.org.uk/research-and-information/research+summaries/cameron.html.

Christie, F. & Derewianka, B. (2010). *School Discourse: Learning to Write Across Years of Schooling*. London: A & C Black.

Collier, V. & Thomas, W. (1997). *School Effectiveness for Language Minority Students*. Available at: http://www.thomasandcollier.com/assets/1997_thomas-collier97-1.pdf.

Cummins J. (2011). *Identity Texts*. London: Trentham Books.

DCSF (2009). *Ensuring the Attainment of More Advanced Learners of EAL – CPD 5: Bridging Talk and Text*. Available at: http://webarchive.nationalarchives.gov.uk/20110202101215/https://nationalstrategies.standards.dcsf.gov.uk/node/187758.

DCSF (2009). *Ensuring the Attainment of More Advanced Learners of EAL – CPD 6: Reading as a Writer*. Available at: http://webarchive.nationalarchives.gov.uk/20110202131926/https://nationalstrategies.standards.dcsf.gov.uk/node/227032.

DfES (2002). *Grammar for Writing: Supporting Pupils Learning EAL*. Available at: https://www.naldic.org.uk/Resources/NALDIC/Teaching%20and%20Learning/ealgrammar.pdf.

DfES (2004). *Pedagogy and Practice: Developing Reading*. Available at: http://dera.ioe.ac.uk/id/eprint/5677.

Gibbons, P. (1991). *Learning to Learn in a Second Language*. Australia: PETA.

Gibbons, P. (2006). *Bridging Discourses in the ESL Classroom: Students, Teachers and Researchers*. London: Continuum.

Gibbons, P. (2008). 'Challenging pedagogies: More than just good practice?' *NALDIC Quarterly*, 6(2), pp. 4–14.

Halliday, M. A. K. & Martin, J. R. (1993). *Writing Science*. Abingdon: Routledge.

Jewitt, C. & Kress, G. (Eds.) (2003). *Multimodal Literacy*. New York, NY: Peter Lang.

Katzner, K. (2002). *Languages of the World*. Abingdon: Routledge.

Krashen, S. D. (1982). *Principles and Practice of Second Language Acquisition*. Available at: http://www.sdkrashen.com/content/books/principles_and_practice.pdf.

Lunzer, E. & Gardner, K. (1979). *The Effective Use of Reading*. London: Heinemann Educational.

Mercer, N. (2000). *Words and Minds*. Abingdon: Routledge.

Mohan, B. A. Knowledge Framework website. Available at: http://tslater.public.iastate.edu/kf/.

Mohan, B.A. (1986). *Language and Content*. Boston, MA: Addison-Wesley.

Rose, D. & Martin, J. (2012). *Learning to Write, Reading to Learn: Genre, Knowledge and Pedagogy in the Sydney School*. Sheffield: Equinox.

Vygotsky, L. S. (1978). *Mind and Society: The Development of Higher Psychological Processes*. Cambridge, MA: Harvard University Press.